Oliver Optic

Brave Old Salt

Or, life on the quarter deck. A story of the great rebellion

Oliver Optic

Brave Old Salt
Or, life on the quarter deck. A story of the great rebellion

ISBN/EAN: 9783337213176

Printed in Europe, USA, Canada, Australia, Japan

Cover: Foto ©ninafisch / pixelio.de

More available books at **www.hansebooks.com**

Somers and the Admiral. Page 202.

BRAVE OLD SALT;

OR,

LIFE ON THE QUARTER DECK.

A Story of the Great Rebellion.

BY

OLIVER OPTIC,

AUTHOR OF "THE SOLDIER BOY," "THE SAILOR BOY," "THE YOUNG LIEUTENANT"
"THE YANKEE MIDDY," "FIGHTING JOE," "THE WOODVILLE STORIES,"
"THE RIVERDALE STORY BOOKS," ETC., ETC.

BOSTON:
LEE AND SHEPARD, PUBLISHERS.
NEW YORK:
CHARLES T. DILLINGHAM.

TO

SAMUEL C. PERKINS, ESQ.,

This Book

IS RESPECTFULLY DEDICATED,

BY HIS FRIEND

WILLIAM T. ADAMS.

PREFACE.

This volume, the sixth and last of "THE ARMY AND NAVY STORIES," is a record of "Life on the Quarter Deck," mostly in the squadron of Vice Admiral Farragut, one of whose familiar appellations, used in the ward-room and on the berth deck, has furnished the leading title of the book. The terrible war which devastated our country for four years has given to history two generals, Grant and Sherman, and one admiral, Farragut, whose achievements are unsurpassed, if they are equalled, in the annals of military and naval warfare; but while the author, in this work, has gratefully rendered his tribute of admiration to the distinguished naval commander, he has not attempted to present a complete biography of him.

Those who have read the preceding volumes of this series need hardly be told that this is a book of adventure — of personal experience in the great struggle of the nineteenth century. Jack Somers, "The Sailor Boy," Mr. Somers, "The Yankee Middy," and Captain Somers, Lieutenant Commanding, are the same person; though often as he changes his official position, he is still the same honest, true, and Christian young man.

In our completed sixth volume we take leave of the Somers

family with many regrets. If our young friends in the army and navy had been less true, noble, and Christian, we could have parted with less sorrow. Yet the army and navy, as they crushed the Rebellion, have given us many young men just as true, just as noble and Christian. Let us gratefully cherish these living heroes, and they will not pass away from us "like a tale that is told."

To the readers, young and old, who have perseveringly followed my heroes through the two thousand pages of this series, I am even more than grateful; for I feel that they have sympathized with me in my desire to present a lofty ideal to the young man of to-day — one who will be true to God, true to himself, and true to his country, in whatever sphere his lot may be cast, whether on the forecastle or the quarter deck; as a private or an officer, in the great army which must ever battle with life's trials and temptations till the crown immortal be won.

WILLIAM T. ADAMS.

Harrison Square, Mass., March 13, 1866.

CONTENTS.

CHAPTER		PAGE
I.	LIEUTENANT PILLGRIM.	11
II.	WAITING FOR THE SHIP.	23
III.	THE WOUNDED SAILOR.	33
IV.	THE FRONT CHAMBER.	44
V.	SOMERS COMES TO HIS SENSES.	55
VI.	LIEUTENANT WYNKOOP, R. N.	66
VII.	LANGDON'S LETTERS.	77
VIII.	THE UNITED STATES STEAMER CHATAUQUA.	87
IX.	IN THE STATE-ROOM.	97
X.	THE CHIEF CONSPIRATOR.	108
XI.	AFTER GENERAL QUARTERS.	119
XII.	THE BEN NEVIS.	130
XIII.	A CONFLICT OF AUTHORITY.	140
XIV.	THE PRIZE STEAMER.	150
XV.	THE PRISONER IN THE CABIN.	160
XVI.	CAPTAIN WALMSLEY.	170
XVII.	OFF MOBILE BAY.	180
XVIII.	BRAVE OLD SALT.	190
XIX.	THE BOAT EXPEDITION.	200
XX.	THE PICKET BOAT.	211
XXI.	THE BEN LOMOND.	222

XXII.	RUNNING THE BLOCKADE.	233
XXIII.	A YANKEE TRICK.	244
XXIV.	PILLGRIM AND LANGDON.	254
XXV.	THE BATTLE OF MOBILE BAY.	264
XXVI.	IN THE HOSPITAL.	274
XXVII.	MISS PORTINGTON NOT AT HOME.	284
XXVIII.	THE BEN LEDI.	294
XXIX.	A LONG CHASE.	303
XXX.	THE END OF THE REBELLION.	318

BRAVE OLD SALT.

BRAVE OLD SALT;

OR,

LIFE ON THE QUARTER DECK.

CHAPTER I.

LIEUTENANT PILLGRIM.

"WELL, Prodigy, I congratulate you on your promotion. I even agree with your enthusiastic admirers, who say that no young man better deserves his advancement than you," said Miss Kate Portington, standing in the entry of her father's house at Newport, holding Mr. Ensign John Somers by the hand.

"Thank you, Miss Portington," replied the young officer, with a blush caused as much by the excitement of that happy moment, as by the handsome compliment paid by the fair girl, who, we are compelled to acknowledge, had formed no inconsiderable portion of the young man's thoughts, hopes, and aspirations during the preceding year.

John Somers had been examined by the board of naval officers appointed for the purpose, had been triumphantly passed, and promoted to the rank he now held. A short furlough had been granted to him, and he had just come from Pinchbrook, where he had spent a week. A visit to Newport was now almost as indispensable as one to the home of his childhood, and on his way to join the ship to which he had been ordered, he paused to discharge this pleasing duty.

Ensign Somers was dressed in a new uniform, and a certain boyish look, for which he was partly indebted to the short jacket he had worn as a midshipman, had vanished. Perhaps Miss Portington felt that the pertness, not to say impudence, with which she had formerly treated him, though allowable, under a liberal toleration, towards a boy, would hardly be justifiable in her intercourse with a young man. Though, from the force of habit, she called him "Prodigy," there was a certain maidenly reserve in her manner, which rather puzzled Somers, and he could not help asking himself what he had done to cause this slight chill in her tones and actions.

Undoubtedly it was the frock coat which produced this refrigerating effect; but it was a very elegant and well-fashioned garment, having the shoulder straps on which glistened the "foul anchor," indicating his new rank, and each sleeve being adorned with a single gold band on the cuff, also indicative of his new position. The cap, which he now held in his hand, was decorated with a band of gold lace, and bore on its front the appropriate naval emblem. In strict accordance with the traditions of the navy, he wore kid gloves, without which a naval officer, on a ceremonial occasion, would be as incomplete as a ship without a rudder.

We have no means of knowing what Mr. Ensign Somers thought of himself in his "new rig," which certainly fitted with admirable nicety, and gave him an appearance of maturity which he did not possess when we last saw him on the quarter deck of the Rosalie. We will venture to assert, however, that he felt like a man, and fully believed that he was one — a commendable sentiment in a person of his years, inasmuch as, if he feels like a man, he is the more likely to act like one. As we can hardly suppose he soared above all the vanities of his impressible period of life, it is more than probable that he regarded himself as a very good looking young fellow; which brilliant suggestion was, no doubt, wholly or in part due to the new uniform he wore.

If not wholly above the weakness of a young man of twenty, possibly he had a great deal of confidence in his own knowledge and ability, regarded some of the veterans of the navy as "old fogies," and looked upon his own father as "a slow coach." But we must do Mr. Somers the justice to say that he tried to be humble in his estimate of himself, and to bear the honors he had won with meekness; that he endeavored to crush down and mortify that overweening self-sufficiency which distorts and disfigures the character of many estimable young men. His native bashfulness had, in some measure, been overcome by his intercourse with the world, and the humility of his nature, though occasionally assaulted by the accident of a new coat and an extra supply of gold lace, or by the hearty commendations of his superiors, was genuine, and, in the main, saved him from the besetting sin of his years.

Standing in the presence of Miss Kate Portington, after an absence of several months, wearing a new coat glittering with the laurels he had won on the bloodstained decks of the nation's ships, he would have been more than human if he had not felt proud of what he was, and what he had done — proud, not vain. He was happy, holding the hand of her who had occupied so large a place in his thoughts, and whose image had fringed with roseate hues his brightest hopes and strongest aspirations.

Kate was not so free with him as she had been, and her reserve annoyed and perplexed him. He had anticipated a much warmer welcome than that which greeted him on his arrival. He was slightly disappointed, though there was nothing in her manner for which he could have reproached her, even if their relations had been more intimate than they were. She was less stormy, but still gentle and kind; a little more distant in manner, though her looks and words assured him she regarded him with undiminished interest. Had he known that the elegant frock coat he wore produced the chill in the lady which so vexed and disconcerted him, he would willingly have exchanged it for the short jacket in which he had won his promotion.

They were standing in the entry. When the servant admitted Mr. Somers, Kate had heard his voice, and perhaps from prudential motives — for there was a visitor in the parlor — she had preferred to meet him in the hall.

"You have been very fortunate, Mr. Somers," added she, gently releasing her hand from that of the ensign.

Mr. Somers, instead of "Prodigy"!

"I have. I don't deserve my promotion, I know; but I could not help taking it when it was within my reach," replied Somers; and her words, though so slightly chilled that the frigid tone could not have been noticed by any one who did not expect an unreasonable warmth, took half the conceit out of him, and let him down a long reach from the high hopes and brilliant expectations with which he had looked forward to this meeting.

"On the contrary, Mr. Somers, I think you deserve even more than you have received."

"Thank you, Miss Portington; you were always more lavish of kind words than I deserved."

"Why, Prodigy—"

She suddenly checked herself. It was evident to Somers that she intended to say something pert or saucy. Perhaps she choked down the impertinent words from the fear that the honorable secretary of the navy, if such wild and wayward young ladies as herself were permitted to contaminate the plushy air of Newport society, would remove the Naval Academy back to Annapolis, where it is better to be "proper" than to be loyal.

"You were about to say something, Miss Portington," said Somers.

"I was, but it was saucy."

"I am sorry you did not say it."

"I am glad I did not, for you must know, Mr. Somers, that mother has scolded me so much for being saucy, that I have solemnly resolved to be proper in all things henceforth and forevermore."

"I am sorry for it," answered Somers, with unaffected earnestness.

"Sorry, you wretch?"

Somers laughed.

"There's another slip. I have done my best to reform my life. I am afraid I shall never succeed. Now, Prodigy—"

Somers laughed again.

"Again!" exclaimed Kate.

"I wish to ask one favor of you, Miss Portington."

"It would afford me more pleasure to grant it, than it does you to ask it. Name it."

"That you will never call me Prodigy again."

"I had firmly resolved before you came never to do it," laughed she.

"Well, I only asked it in order to help along your good resolutions."

"Then you are making fun of me?"

"Like yourself, I am very serious."

"But I am in earnest, Mr. Somers; I mean to reform. Now, father and mother will be very glad to see you, Mr. Somers."

"Your father?"

"He was temporarily relieved to attend a court martial. He is going away again to-morrow."

"You have other visitors?"

"Only Lieutenant Pillgrim."

"I have not the pleasure of his acquaintance."

"He is a Virginian, I believe; at any rate he is from the South, and has just been restored to his rank in the navy."

Kate led the way into the parlor, where he was first welcomed by her mother.

"Mr. Somers, I am glad to see you, and to congratulate you on your promotion," said the commodore, as he grasped the hand of the young officer.

"Thank you, sir," replied Somers. "The only ungratified wish I had was that I might be appointed to your ship."

"My ship!"

"I should have been glad to serve under so able and distinguished a commander."

"I wouldn't have you in my ship," promptly returned the commodore, shaking his head energetically.

Somers looked abashed, and Kate wore a troubled expression.

"I should endeavor to do my duty," he added.

"I have no doubt of it, but I wouldn't have you in my ship."

"Your remark is not very complimentary," said Somers, his face beginning to flush with indignation at what seemed to be an assault upon his professional character.

"It is the most complimentary thing I could say to you. And I mean what I say: I wouldn't have you in my ship."

"Why not, father?" demanded Kate.

"Because I like the young dog, and because I believe in discipline. I never indulge in partiality on board my ship, and it is better to keep out of temptation. I am under obligations to you, Mr. Somers; I am happy to acknowledge them, but they must not come between me and duty. Mr. Somers, Lieutenant Pillgrim," continued Commodore Portington, turning to the visitor.

Somers looked at the officer thus indicated, and as his

eyes rested upon him, he started back with a momentary astonishment, for the face had a strange look of familiarity to him.

"Mr. Somers, I am happy to meet and to know you. Your name and reputation are already familiar to me."

"I am glad to know you, sir," replied Somers, with some confusion. "Your face looks so familiar to me, that I think we must have met before."

"Never, to my knowledge," answered the lieutenant, with easy self-possession.

"I was quite sure I had seen you before."

"Possibly; I do not remember it, however."

"If I had met you without the favor of an introduction, I should certainly have claimed the honor of your acquaintance."

"I should have been proud to be so claimed, but I must confess you would have had the advantage of me."

"Of course, I must be mistaken, as you suggest."

"It is not unlikely that we have met in some anteroom where we were dancing attendance on the powers that be, in search of employment; but I am quite sure, Mr. Somers, that I should have been proud and happy to number you among my friends."

"It is not too late now," said the commodore.

"Certainly not. I should be but too happy to have as my friend one who has served his country so faithfully," added Mr. Pillgrim, as he bowed gracefully to

Somers, "especially as I understand we are appointed to the same ship."

"Indeed!"

"I am ordered to the Chatauqua."

"So am I."

"Then, Mr. Pillgrim, you will take care of our Prodigy; you will be excellent friends, I trust," said Kate, beginning very impulsively in her old way, and suddenly checking herself when her resolution to be "proper" interposed itself.

"What is the matter, Kate? Have you and Mr. Somers had a falling out?" demanded the commodore.

"O, no, father."

"You talk as though you had had a quarrel, and for a moment had forgotten to be savage."

"We have had no quarrel, pa," replied Kate, blushing. "I was going to be saucy, but ma says I must not be saucy, and I shall not be saucy any more. I only hoped the two gentlemen who are going to live together in the same ship would be good friends."

"Of course they will. Officers never quarrel."

"Perhaps they don't; but they are not always as good friends as I hope these gentlemen will be," laughed Kate.

"Perhaps he will be my friend for your sake, if he is not for mine," added Pillgrim.

"I do not wish that. I don't like to have anybody do anything for my sake, unless it be to take paregoric when I am sick."

"I trust I shall not be paregoric to him," said Pillgrim.

"Then he will not take you for my sake."

"As Lieutenant Pillgrim is my superior officer, I should be likely to court his good will, and prize his friendship very highly. If we are not friends, I am sure it will not be my fault."

At this moment the dinner bell rang; and although Somers did not feel intimate enough with the family to invite himself to dine, he was easily prevailed upon to remain, and gallantly gave his arm to Mrs. Portington, as Kate, for some wayward reason of her own, had already seized upon that of Lieutenant Pillgrim.

At the table Somers sat opposite the lieutenant, and he found it impossible to avoid looking upon him with a strange and undefinable interest. Since his first glance at the commodore's visitor, who seemed to be on the best of terms with the family, he had been perplexed by some strange misgivings. He could not banish from his mind an assurance that he had seen him before; that he had talked with him, and even been, to some extent, intimate with him.

The thought that Kate was somewhat changed in her demeanor towards him did not contribute to increase his satisfaction. She had contrived to take the lieutenant's arm instead of his own, and perhaps he had come as the successor of Phil Kennedy, who had been reputed to be high in her good graces. But Mr. Pillgrim was a gentleman of thirty-five, at least, and this was not probable, in his view of the matter. Somers, being disinterested, was more worried to know when, where, and under what circumstances he had met the lieutenant.

CHAPTER II.

WAITING FOR THE SHIP.

SOMERS was utterly unable to satisfy himself in regard to Lieutenant Pillgrim. The face was certainly familiar to him, not as a combination of remembered features, but rather as an expression. To him the eye seemed to be the whole of the man, and its gaze would haunt him, though his memory refused to identify it with any time, place, or circumstances. Though his reason compelled him to believe that he was mistaken, and that Mr. Pillgrim was actually a stranger, his consciousness of having seen, and even of having been intimate with, the gentleman, most obstinately refused to be shaken.

"Of course, gentlemen, you have no idea to what point the Chatauqua has been ordered?" said the commodore.

"I have not," replied Mr. Pillgrim.

"I have heard it said that she was going to the Gulf," added Somers.

"Very likely; there are two points where extensive naval operations are likely to be undertaken — at Mobile and at Wilmington. The rebellion has had so many hard knocks that the bottom must drop out before many months."

"I am afraid the end is farther off than most people at the North are willing to believe," said Mr. Pillgrim.

"Every thing looks hopeful. If we can contrive to batter down Fort Fisher, and open Mobile Bay, the rebels may count the months of their Confederacy on their fingers."

"I think there is greater power of resistance left in the South, than we give it the credit for."

"The rebels have fought well; what of it?" continued the commodore, who did not seem to be pleased with the style of the lieutenant's remarks.

"As fighting men, we can hardly fail to respect those who have fought so bravely as the people of the South."

"People of the South!" sneered the commodore. "Why don't you call them rebels?"

"Of course that is what I mean," answered Mr. Pillgrim, a slight flush visible on his cheek.

"If you mean it, why don't you say it? Call things by their right names. The people of the South are not all rebels. Why, confound it, Farragut is a Southerner; so is General Anderson; so are a hundred men, who have distinguished themselves in putting down treason. It's an insult to these men to talk about the people of the South as rebels."

"I agree with you, Commodore Portington, and what I said was only a form of expression."

"It's a very bad form of expression. Why, man, you are a Southerner yourself."

"I am; and I suppose that is what makes me so proud of the good fighting the people of the South — I mean the rebels — have done. We can't help respecting men who have behaved with so much gallantry."

"Can't we?" exclaimed the commodore, with a sneer so wholesome and honest, that Lieutenant Pillgrim withered under it. "I can help it. I have no respect for rebels and traitors under any circumstances."

"Nor I, as rebels and traitors," replied Pillgrim, mildly.

"As rebels and traitors! I don't like these fine-spun distinctions. If a man is a traitor, call him so, and swing him up on the fore-yard arm, where he belongs."

"You are willing to acknowledge that the rebels have fought well in this war?" added the lieutenant.

"They have fought well: I don't deny it."

"And you appreciate gallant conduct?"

"That depends on the cause. No, sir! I don't appreciate gallant conduct on the part of rebels and traitors. It is not gallant conduct; and the better they fight, the more wicked they are."

"I can hardly take your view of the case."

"Can't you? The best fighting I ever saw in my life

was on the deck of a pirate ship. The black-hearted villains fought like demons. Not a man of them would yield the breadth of a hair. We had to cut them down like dogs. Is piracy respectable because these men fought well?"

"Certainly not; but the bravery of such men —"

"Nonsense! I know what you are going to say; but you can't separate the pirate from his piracy, nor the traitor from his treason," replied the commodore, warmly. "The other day I saw a little dirty urchin fighting with his mother. The young cub had run away, I suppose, and the woman was dragging him back to the house. He was not more than six years old, but he displayed a power of resistance which rather astonished me. He kicked, bit, scratched, and yelled like a young tiger. He called his mother everything but a lady. The poor woman tugged at him with all her strength, but the little rascal was almost a match for her. I wanted to take him by the nape of the neck, and shake the ugly out of him; nothing but my fixed principles of neutrality prevented me from doing so. I suppose, Mr. Pillgrim, you would have sympathized with the brat, because he fought bravely."

"Hardly," replied the lieutenant, laughing at the simile.

"But he fought like a tiger, and displayed no mean strategy in his rebellious warfare. Of course he was worthy of your admiration," sneered the commodore.

"That's hardly a fair comparison."

"The fairest in the world. The rebels have insulted their own mother — the parent that fostered, protected, and loved them. They undertook to run away from her; and when she attempts to bring them back to their duty, they kick, and scratch, and bite; and you admire them because they fight well."

"I stand convicted, Commodore Portington. I never took this view of the matter; I acknowledge that you are right," said Mr. Pillgrim.

Somers, who had been an attentive listener to the conversation, thought the lieutenant yielded very gracefully, and much more readily than could have been expected; but then the logician was a commodore, and perhaps it was prudence and politeness on his part to agree with his powerful superior.

After dinner the party took a ride to the beach and to the Glen; and after an early tea, Somers and Pillgrim, who were to be fellow-passengers to Philadelphia, where the Chatauqua was fitting out, began to demonstrate in the direction of their departure. Kate, though she had been tolerably playful during the afternoon, had, in the main, carried out her good resolution to be proper. She had not been impudent — hardly pert; and deprived of this convenient mask for whatever kindness she might have entertained towards the young ensign, she seemed to be very cold and indifferent to him. She was more thoughtful, serious, and earnest than when they had met on former occasions. He could not help asking himself what he had done to produce this marked change in her conduct.

"Good by, Miss Portington," said he, when he had taken leave of her father and mother.

"Good by, Mr. Somers. Shall I hear from you when you reach your station?" she asked, presenting her hand.

"If you desire it."

"If I desire it! Why, Mr. Somers, you forget that I am deeply interested in your success."

"Perhaps, if I do anything of which you would care to learn, the newspapers may inform you of the fact," replied Somers, with a kind of grim smile, which seemed actually to alarm poor Kate.

"I would rather hear it from you."

"I judge that you are more interested in my success than you are in me."

"Ah, Mr. Somers, you cannot separate the pirate from his piracy, pa said; nor the hero from his heroism, let me add."

"Thank you, Miss Portington."

"I cannot forget how deeply indebted we are to you, Mr. Somers."

"I wish you could."

"Why do you wish so?" demanded the astonished maiden; more astonished at his manner than his words.

"I am sorry to have you burdened with such a weight of obligation."

"I think you mean to quarrel with me, Mr. Somers. I beg you will not be so savage just as you are going away," laughed Kate, though there was a troubled expression on her fair face. "I asked you if I should hear from you, Mr. Somers."

"Certainly, if you desire."

"Why do you qualify your words? I should be just as glad to hear from you as I ever was."

"Then you shall, at every opportunity."

"Thank you, Mr. Somers. That sounds hearty and honest, as father would say."

"I do not wish you to feel an interest in me from a sense of duty. I shall not write any letters from a sense of duty, or even because I have promised to do so. I shall write to you because — because I can't help it," stammered Somers, almost overcome by the violence of his exertions.

"I thank you, Mr. Somers, and I am sure your letters will be all the more welcome from my knowledge of the fact."

"Good by," said he, gently pressing the little hand he held.

"Good by," she replied; and to his great satisfaction and delight, the pressure was returned — a kind of tele-

3 *

graphic signal, infinitely more expressive than all the words in the spelling-book, strung into sentences, could have been to a young man in his desperate condition.

Mr. Ensign Somers was now entirely satisfied. That gentle pressure of the hand had atoned for all her reserve and coldness, real or imaginary, and made the future bright and pleasant to look upon. Undoubtedly Mr. Somers was a silly young fellow; but there is some consolation in believing that he was just like all young men under similar circumstances.

Mr. Pillgrim followed him out of the house, and they hastened down to the wharf to take the steamer for New York. On the passage the two officers treated each other with courtesy and consideration, but there appeared to be no strong sympathy of thought or feeling between them, and they were not drawn so closely together as they might have been under similar circumstances, if there had been more of opinion and sentiment common between them.

On their arrival at Philadelphia, they found the Chatauqua was still in the hands of the workmen, and would not go into commission for a week or ten days. They reported to the commandant of the navy yard, and took up their quarters at the "Continental," where Somers found his old friend Mr. Waldron, who had been detached from the Ro·alie at his own request, and ordered to the Chatauqua, in which he was to serve as executive officer. This was splendid news to Somers, for he regarded Mr. Waldron as a true and trusty friend, in whom he could with safety confide.

"Do you know Lieutenant Pillgrim?" asked Somers, after they had discussed their joint information in regard to the new ship.

"I am not personally acquainted with him, though I have heard his name mentioned. He is a Virginian, I think."

"Yes."

"If I mistake not, there were some doubts about his loyalty, though he never tendered his resignation; he has been kept in the background."

"He seems to be a loyal and true man."

"No doubt of it, or he would not have been appointed to the Chatauqua."

"He has some respect for the rebels, but no sympathy."

"I think he has frequently applied for employment, but has not obtained it until the present time. I have no doubt he is a good fellow and a good officer. He ranks next to me. But, Somers, I leave town in half an hour," continued Mr. Waldron, consulting his watch. "I am going to run home for a few days, till the ship goes into commission. I will see you here on my return."

Somers walked to the railroad station with his late commander, and parted with him as the train started. During the three succeeding days, he visited the museums, libraries, and other places of resort, interesting to a young man of his tastes. He went to the navy yard every day, and, with his usual zeal, learned what he could of the build, rig, and armament of the Chatauqua, and gathered such other information relating to his profession as would be useful to him in the future.

Lieutenant Pillgrim passed his time in a different manner. Though he was not what the world would call an intemperate or an immoral man, he spent many of his hours in bar-rooms, billiard-saloons, and places of public amusement. He several times invited Somers to "join" him at the bar, to play at billiards, and to visit the theatre, and other places of more questionable morality. The young officer was not a prude, but he never drank, did not know how to play billiards, and never visited a gambling resort. He went to the theatre two or three times; but this was the limit of his indulgence.

Mr. Pillgrim was courteous and gentlemanly; he did not press his invitations. He treated his brother officer with the utmost kindness and consideration; was always ready, and even forward, to serve him; and their relations were of the pleasantest character.

One evening, when Somers called at the office for the key of his room, after his return from the navy yard, a letter was handed to him. The writing was an unfamiliar hand, scrawling and hardly legible. It was evidently the production of an illiterate person. On reaching his room he opened it.

CHAPTER III.

THE WOUNDED SAILOR.

THE curiosity of Somers was not a little excited before he opened the uncouth letter in his hand. It was postmarked Philadelphia, which made its reception all the more strange, for he had no friends or acquaintances residing in the city. He tore open the dirty epistle, which was not even enclosed in an envelope, and read as follows : —

PHILA. June the 19. 1864.

MR. JOHN SOMERS ESQ. Sir. I been wounded in the leg up the Missippi and can not do nothing more. I been in your division aboard the Rosalie. and I know you was a good man and I know you was a good officer, I hope you be in good helth, as I am not at this present writen. my Leg is very bad, and don't git no better. This is to inform you that I am the only son of a poor widdow, who has no other Son, and she can not do nothing for me, nor I can't do nothing for her. I have Fout for my countrey and have been woundded in the servis.

If you could git a penshin for me. it would be a grate help to me Sorrowin condition. I live No — Front Street. If I might make bold to ask you to come and see a old Sailor, thrown on the beam ends of missfortune, I would be very thankful to you.

    Yours to command,
      THOMAS BARRON.

N. B. The doctor says he thinks my Leg will have to come off.

Tom Longstone knows me, and you ask him, he will tell you all About me.

"Thomas Barron," mused Somers, as he folded the letter. "I don't remember him. There were two or three Toms on board the Rosalie. At any rate, I have nothing better to do than call upon him. He is an old sailor, and that is enough for me."

It was already after dark; but he decided to visit the sufferer that night, and after tea he left the house for this purpose. He was sufficiently acquainted with the streets of this systematic city to make his way without assistance. Of course he did not expect to find the home of the old sailor in a wealthy and aristocratic portion of the city; but if he had understood the character of the section to which the direction led him, he would probably have deferred his charitable mission till the following day. On reaching the vicinity of the place indicated, he found himself in a vile locality, surrounded by the lowest and most depraved of the population.

With considerable difficulty he found the number mentioned in the letter. The lower story of the building was occupied as a liquor shop, and a further examination of the premises assured him the place was a sailor's boarding-house. As this fact was not inconsistent with the character of Tom Barron, he entered the shop. Half a dozen vagabonds had possession; and as Somers entered, the attention of the whole group was directed to him.

"Is there a sailor by the name of Thomas Barron in this house?" asked Somers of the greasy, corpulent woman, who stood behind about four feet of counter, forming the bar, on which were displayed several bottles and decanters.

"Yes, sir; and very bad he is too," replied the woman, civilly enough, though the young officer could hardly help shuddering in her presence.

"Could I see him?"

"I 'spect you can, if you be the officer Tom says is comin' to see him."

"I am the person."

"Tom's very bad."

"So he says in his letter."

"He hain't had a minute's peace or comfort with that leg sence he come home from the war. Be you any relation of his?"

"I am not."

"Mebbe you're his friend."

"He served under me in the Rosalie."

"Tom hain't paid no board for two months, which comes hard on a poor woman like me, takin' care of him, and his mother too, that come here to nuss him."

"Perhaps something can be done for him."

"Well, I hope so. I don't see how I can keep him any longer. He owes me forty dollars. If any body'll pay half on't, I'd keep on doin' for him."

"I will see what can be done for him. Why was he not sent to the hospital?"

"He's too bad to be sent, and he don't want to go, nuther. He says the doctors try speriments on poor fellers like him, and he don't want to be cut up afore he's dead."

"Well, I will endeavor to have something done for him. I am entirely willing to help him as much as I can."

"Perhaps you'd be willin' to do sunthin' towards payin' my bill, then."

"Perhaps I will; but I wish to see the man before I do anything. Will you show me to his room?"

"I don't go up and down stairs none now. Here, Childs, you show this gentleman up to the front room," said the landlady to one of the vagabonds before her. "Then go and tell Tom his officer has come. I suppose they'll want to slick up a little, afore they let you in; but Miss Barron will tell you when she is ready."

Somers followed the man up a flight of rickety stairs, and was ushered into the front room. It was a bedchamber, supplied with the rudest and coarsest furniture. The visitor sat down, after telling Childs that the sailor's mother need not stop to "slick up" before he was admitted. He did not like the surroundings, even independent of the villanous odors that rose from the groggery, and those that were engendered in the apartment where he sat. Slush and tar were agreeable perfumes, compared with those which assaulted his sense in this chamber; and he hoped Mrs. Barron would humiliate her pride to an extent which would permit him to make a speedy exit from the house.

Mrs. Barron, however, appeared not to be in a hurry, and Somers waited ten minutes by his watch, which seemed to expand into a full hour before he heard a sound to disturb the monotony of the chamber's quiet. But when it was disturbed, it was in such a manner that he forgot all about the place and the odors, the hour and the occasion, and even the poor sailor, who had so piteously appealed to him for assistance.

In the rear of the room in which Somers sat, there was a door communicating with another apartment. The house was old and out of repair; and this door, never very nicely adjusted, was now warped and thrown out of place, so that great cracks yawned around the edges, and whatever was said or done in one room, of which any knowledge could be obtained by the sense of hearing, was immediately patent to the occupants of the other. Somers heard footsteps in the rear room, though the parties appeared not to have come up the stairs by which he had ascended. The rattling of chairs and of glass ware next saluted his ears; but as yet Somers had not the slightest interest in the business of the adjoining apartment, and only wished that Mrs. Barron would speedily complete the preparations for his reception.

"It's dangerous business," said one of the men in the rear room; which remark followed a smack of the lips, and a rude depositing of the glass on the table, indicating that the speaker had just swallowed his dram.

The man uttered his remark in a loud tone, exhibiting a strange carelessness, if the matter in hand was as dangerous as the words implied.

"I know it is dangerous, Langdon," said another person, in a voice which instantly riveted the attention of the listener.

Somers heard the voice. It startled him, and he had no eye, ear, or thought for anything but the individual who had last spoken. If he had considered his position at all, it would only have been to wish that Mrs. Barron might be as proud as a Chestnut Street belle, in order to afford him time to inform himself in relation to the business of the men who occupied the other room.

"You have been shut up in Fort Lafayette once," added the first speaker.

"In a good cause I am willing to go again," replied the voice so familiar to the ears of Somers. "I lost eighty thousand dollars in a venture just like this. I must get my money back."

"If you can, Coles."

Coles! But Somers did not need to have his identity confirmed by the use of his name. He knew Coles's voice. At Newport he had lain in the fore-sheets of the academy boat, and heard Coles and Phil Kennedy mature their plan to place the Snowden on the ocean, as a Confederate cruiser. He had listened to the whole conversation on that occasion, and the knowledge he had thus obtained enabled the government to capture the steamer, and defeat the intentions of the conspirators.

The last Somers had known of Coles, he was a prisoner in Fort Lafayette. Probably he had been released by the same influence which set Phil Kennedy at liberty, and permitted him to continue his career of treason and plunder. Coles had lost eighty thousand dollars by his speculation in the Snowden, for one half of which Kennedy was holden to him; but the bond had been effectually cancelled by the death of the principal. Coles wanted his money back. It was a very natural desire;

but Somers could not help considering it as a very extravagant one, under present circumstances.

The listener could not help regarding it as a most remarkable thing, that he should again be within hearing of Coles, engaged in plotting treason. Such an event might happen once; but that it should occur a second time was absolutely marvellous. If our readers are of the opinion that the writer is too severely taxing their credulity in imposing the situation just described upon them, he begs they will suspend their judgment till the sequel justifies him.

It was so strange to Somers, that he could not help thinking he had been brought there by some mysterious power to listen to and defeat the intentions of the conspirators. He was not so far wrong as he might have been. It was Coles who spoke; it was Coles who had been in Fort Lafayette; and it was Coles who had lost eighty thousand dollars by the Snowden. All these things were real, and Somers had no suspicion that he had inhaled some of the vile compounds in the bar below, which might have thrown him into a stupor wherein he dreamed the astounding situation in which he was actually placed.

Somers listened, and when Coles had mixed and drank his dram, he spoke again.

"I can and will get my money back," said he, with an oath which froze the blood of the listener.

"Don't believe it, Coles."

"You know me, Langdon," added the plotter, with a peculiar emphasis.

Langdon acknowledged that he did know him; and as there was, therefore, no need of an introduction, Coles proceeded.

"You know me, Langdon; I don't make any mistakes myself."

Perhaps Langdon knew it; but Somers had some doubts, which, however, he did not purpose to urge on this occasion.

"Phil Kennedy was a fool," added Coles, with another oath. "He spoiled all my plans before, and I was glad when I heard that he was killed, though I lost forty thousand dollars when he slipped out. He spilt the milk for me."

Somers thought not.

"Phil was smart about some things; but he couldn't keep a hotel. Why, that young pup that finally gave him his quietus, twirled him around his fingers, like he had been a school girl."

"Thank you, Mr. Coles; but I shall have the pleasure of serving you in the same way before many weeks," thought Somers, flattered by this warm and disinterested tribute to his strategetic ability.

"You mean Somers?" said Langdon.

"I mean Somers. The young pup isn't twenty-one

yet, but he is the smartest man in the old navy, by all odds, whether the others be admirals, commodores, lieutenants, or what not."

"That's high praise, Coles."

"It's true. If he wasn't an infernal Yankee, I would drink his health in this old Bourbon. Good liquor — isn't it, Langdon?"

"Like the juice of a diamond."

"I would give more for this Somers than I would for any four rear admirals. He has just been appointed to the Chatauqua; but he will be in command of some small craft down South, before many months, doing more mischief to us than any four first-class steamers in the service. He is as brave as a young lion; knows a ship from keel to truck, and is as familiar with every bolt and pin of an engine as though he had been a machinist all his life."

"Big thing, eh, Coles?"

"If I had this Somers, I could make his fortune and mine in a year, and have a million surplus besides."

"What would you do with him?"

"I would give him the command of my steamer. I would rather have him in that place than all the old grannies in the Confederate navy."

Somers thought Mr. Coles was rather extravagant. He had no idea that Mr. Ensign Somers was one tenth part of the man which the amiable and patronizing Mr.

Coles declared he was; and he was impatient to have the speaker announce his intentions, rather than waste any more time in such unwarrantable commendation.

But instead of telling what he intended to do, he confined himself most provokingly to what he had failed to do, giving Langdon minute details of the capture of the Theban and the Snowden, dwelling with peculiar emphasis on the agency of Somers in the work. This was not interesting to the listener, but something better soon followed.

CHAPTER IV.

THE FRONT CHAMBER.

UT I am going to get back the money I lost, and make a pile besides," said Coles, when he had fully detailed the events attending the loss of the Snowden.

"If you can," added the sceptical Langdon.

"Of course there is some risk, but my plans are so well laid that a failure is hardly possible," continued Coles.

"It was possible before."

"Nothing but an accident could have defeated my plan before. Everything worked to my satisfaction, and I was sure of success."

"But you failed."

"I shall not fail again."

"I hope not."

"Then believe I shall not," retorted Coles, apparently irritated by the doubts and fears of his companion.

"It is not safe to believe too much," added Langdon, with a kind of chuckle, whose force Somers could hardly understand; "you believed too much before."

"I have been more cautious this time, and I wouldn't give anybody five per cent. to insure the venture."

Somers was becoming very impatient to hear the particulars of the plan, for he was in momentary fear of being summoned to the bedside of the wounded sailor. Coles was most provokingly deliberate in the discussion of his treasonable project; but when the naval officer considered that the conversation was not especially intended for him, he did not very severely censure the conspirators for their tardiness.

"I don't understand what your plan is," said Langdon.

"Nor I either," was Somers's facetious thought.

"I will tell you all about it. Are there any ears within hail of us?"

"Not an ear."

"Is there anybody in the front room?"

"No."

"Are you sure?"

"The old woman told me the front room was not occupied. She sent in there an officer who wanted to see a sick sailor up stairs; but he is gone before this time."

"Perhaps not; make sure on this point before I open my mouth. I have no idea of being tripped up this time," said the cautious Coles.

"I will look into the front room," added Langdon, "though I know there is no one there."

Somers was rather annoyed at this demonstration of prudence; but it was quite natural, and he was all the more interested to hear the rest of the conference. Dismissing for a moment the dignity of the quarter deck, he dropped hastily on the floor, and crawled under the bed, concluding that Langdon, who was already fully satisfied the front room was empty, would not push his investigations to an unreasonable extent. But he had already prepared himself for the worst, and if his presence were detected, he resolved to take advantage of the high estimation in which he was held, and, for his country's good, proposed to offer his valuable services in getting the piratical ship to sea. He could thus obtain the secret, and defeat the purposes of the conspirators.

He fortunately avoided the necessity of resorting to this disagreeable course, for Langdon only opened the door, and glanced into the chamber he occupied.

"The room is empty," he reported to Coles, on his return.

"There are cracks around this door big enough to crawl through. Somebody may go into that room without being heard, and listen to all I say."

"There is no danger."

"But there is danger; and I will not leave the ghost of a chance to be discovered. Langdon, lock that front room, and put the key in your pocket. I must have things perfectly secure before I open my mouth."

Langdon complied with the request of his principal; the door was locked, and Somers, without much doubt or distrust, found his retreat cut off for the present. But, at last, everything was fixed to the entire satisfaction of Coles. The glasses clinked again, indicating that the worthies had fortified themselves with another dose from the bottle. Somers crawled out from under the bed, and heedless of the dust which whitened his new uniform, placed himself in a comfortable position, where he could hear all that was said by the confederates.

Coles now told his story in a straightforward, direct manner, and Somers made memoranda on the back of a letter of the principal facts in the statement. The arch conspirator had just purchased a fine iron side-wheel steamer, captured on the blockade, called the Ben Nevis. She was about four hundred tons burden, and under favorable circumstances had often made sixteen knots an hour. It had already been announced in the newspapers that the Ben Nevis would run regularly between New York and St. John. Coles intended to clear her properly for her destined port, where she could, by an arrangement already made, be supplied with guns, ammunition, and a crew. She was to clear regularly for New York, but instead of proceeding there was to commence her piratical course on the ocean.

This was the plan of the worthy Mr. Coles, which Langdon permitted him to develop without a single interruption. But the prudent, or rather critical, confederate raised many objections, which were discussed at great length — so great that Somers, possessed of the principal facts, would have left the room, if the door had not been locked, and escaped from the house, so as to avoid the possibility of being discovered. The wounded sailor could be attended to on the following day.

"But one thing we lack," continued Coles, after he had removed all the objections of his companion.

"More than one, I fear," said the doubtful **Langdon**.

"Well, one thing more than all others."

"What is that?"

"A naval officer to command her."

"There are plenty of them."

"No doubt of it; but they are not the kind I want. I need a man who will play into my hand, as well as grind up the Yankees. I have no idea of burning all the property captured by my vessel."

"Why don't you take command yourself?"

"I have other business to do."

"There are scores of Confederate naval officers in Canada and New Brunswick," suggested Langdon.

"I know them all, and I wouldn't trust them to command a mud-scow. In a word, Langdon, I want this Somers, and I must have him."

"But he is a northern Yankee. He would sooner cut his own throat than engage in such an enterprise."

"Thank you for that," said Somers to himself. "If you had known me all my lifetime, you couldn't have said a better or a truer thing of me."

"I know he is actually reeking with what he calls loyalty. He will be a hard subject, but I think he can be brought over."

"Perhaps he can."

"It must be done; that is the view we must take of the matter."

"It will be easier to believe it than to do it."

"This is to be your share of the enterprise."

"Mine?"

"Yes."

"Well, I think you have given me the biggest job in the work."

"It can be done," said Coles, confidently. "Somers is a mere boy in years, though he is smarter and knows more than any man in the navy in the prime of life."

"I'm afraid he is too smart, and knows too much to be caught in such a scrape."

"No; he is young and ambitious. Offer him a commission as a commander in the Confederate navy, to begin with. I have the commission duly signed by the president of the Confederacy, countersigned by the secretary of the navy, with a blank for the name of the man who receives it, which I am authorized to fill up as I think best. Somers must have this commission."

"If he will take it."

"He will take it. In the old navy he is nothing but a paltry ensign. He has been kept back. His merit has been ignored. He must stand out of the way for numskulls and old fogies. Even if the war should last ten years longer, he could not reach the rank, in that time, which I now tender him. He will at once be offered the command of a fine steamer, and may walk the quarter deck like a king. He is ambitious, and if you approach him in the right way, you can win him over."

Somers listened with interest to this precious scheme. He did not even feel complimented by the exalted opinion which such a man as Coles entertained of him. It would be a pleasant thing for a young man like him to be a commander, and have a fine steamer; but as he could regard only with horror the idea of firing a gun at a vessel bearing the stars and stripes, he was not even tempted by the bait; and he turned his thoughts from it without the necessity of a "Get thee behind me, Satan," in dismissing it.

"Where is this Somers?" asked Langdon.

"He is at the Continental," replied Coles. "He has been appointed fourth lieutenant of the Chatauqua; but what a position for a man of his abilities! He is better qualified to command the ship than the numskull to whom she has been given. Waldron, the first lieutenant, is smart: he ought to be commander; though I think

Somers did all the hard work in Doboy Sound, for which Waldron got the credit, and for which he was promoted. Pillgrim, the second lieutenant, is a renegade Virginian."

"We had some hopes of him, at one time," said Langdon.

"He is worse than a Vermont Yankee now — has been all along, for that matter. I tried to do something with him, but he talked about the old flag, and other bosh of that sort."

"Let him go," added Langdon, with becoming resignation.

"Let him go! He never went. He has always been a Yankee at heart. If the navy department wouldn't trust him, it was their fault, not his, for the South has not had a worse enemy than he since the first gun was fired at Sumter. He is none the better, and all the more dangerous to us, because he gives the South credit for skill and bravery."

Somers was pleased to hear this good account of Lieutenant Pillgrim; not because he had any doubt in regard to his loyalty, but because it confirmed the good impression he had received of his travelling companion. If the conspirators would only have graciously condescended to resolve the doubts in his mind in regard to some indefinite previous acquaintance he had had with the second lieutenant of the Chatauqua, he would have been greatly obliged to them. They did not do this, and Som ers was still annoyed and puzzled by the belief, patent to his consciousness, that he had somewhere been intimate with the "renegade Virginian," before they met at the house of Commodore Portington.

"Now, Langdon, you must contrive to meet Somers, sound him, and bring him over. You must be cautious with him. He is a young man of good morals — never drinks, gambles, or goes to bad places. He is a perfect gentleman in his manners, never swears, and is the pet of the chaplains."

"I think I can manage him."

"I know you can; I have picked you out of a hundred smart fellows for this work."

"How will it do for me to put on a white choker, and approach him as a doctor of divinity."

"You can't humbug him."

"If I can't, why should I try?"

"If you should pretend to be a clergyman, and he smelt the whiskey in your breath, he would set you down as a hypocrite at once."

"That's so," thought Somers.

"He wouldn't listen to a preacher who drank whiskey. He is a fanatic on these points."

Somers could not imagine where Coles had obtained such an intimate knowledge of his views and principles; though, if he wanted his services in the Confederate navy, it was probable he had made diligent inquiries in regard to his opinions and habits.

"I think I could blind him as a D.D., but I am not strenuous."

"You had better get acquainted with him in some other capacity."

"As you please; I will think over the matter, and be ready to make a strike to-morrow morning. What time is it?"

"Quarter past ten."

"So late! I must be off at once."

Somers heard the clatter of glass-ware again, as the conspirators took the parting libation. He listened to their retreating footsteps, heard Langdon return the key, and then began to wonder what had become of Tom Barron and his mother. He had waited more than two hours in the front room, and no summons had come for him to see the wounded sailor. It was very singular, to say the least; but while he was deliberating on the point, a hand was placed on the door of the chamber. The key turned, and a person entered.

Now, Somers had a very strong objection to being seen after what had occurred. If discovered in this room, Coles might see him, and finding his plans discovered, might change them so as to defeat the ends of justice. And the listener felt that, if detected in this apartment by the conspirators, they would not scruple to take his life in order to save themselves and their schemes.

For these reasons Somers decided not to be seen. The person who entered the room was a rough, seafaring man, and evidently intended to sleep there, which Somers was entirely willing he should do, if it could be done without imperilling his personal safety. He therefore crawled under the bed again, as quietly as possible. Unfortunately it was not quietly enough to escape the observation of the lodger, who, not being of the timid sort, seized him by the leg, dragged him out, and with a volley of marine oaths, began to kick him with his heavy boot.

Somers sprang to his feet, and attempted to explain; but the indignant seaman struck him a heavy blow on the head, which felled him senseless on the floor.

CHAPTER V.

SOMERS COMES TO HIS SENSES.

WHEN Somers opened his eyes, about half an hour after the striking event just narrated, and became conscious that he was still in the land of the living, he was lying on the bed in his chamber at the Continental. By his side stood Lieutenant Pillgrim and a surgeon.

"Where am I?" asked the young officer, using the original expression made and provided for occasions of this kind.

"You are here, my dear fellow," replied the lieutenant.

This valuable information seemed to afford the injured party a great deal of consolation, for he looked around the apartment, not wildly, as he would have done if this book were a novel, but with a look of perplexity and dissatisfaction. As Mr. Ensign Somers was eminently a fighting man on all proper occasions, he probably felt displeased with himself to think he had given the stalwart seaman so easy a victory; for he distinctly remembered the affair in which he had been so rudely treated, though there was a great gulf between the past and the present in his recollection.

"How do you feel, Mr. Somers?" asked the surgeon.

"The fact that I feel at all is quite enough for me at the present time, without going into the question as to how I feel," replied the patient, with a sickly smile. "I don't exactly know how I do feel. My ideas are rather confused."

"I should think they might be," added the surgeon. "You have had a hard rap on the head."

"So I should judge, for my brain is rather muddled."

"Does your head pain you?" asked the medical gentleman, placing his hand on the injured part.

"It does not exactly pain me, but it feels rather sore. I think I will get up, and see how that affects me."

Somers got up, and immediately came to the conclusion that he was not very badly damaged; and the surgeon was happy to corroborate his opinion. With the exception of a soreness over the left temple, he felt pretty well. The blow from the iron fist of the burly seaman had stunned him; and the kicks received from the big boots of the assailant had produced sundry black and blue places on his body, which a man not accustomed to hard knocks might have looked upon with suspicion, but to which Somers paid no attention.

The surgeon had carefully examined him before his consciousness returned, and was fully satisfied that he had not been seriously injured. Somers walked across the room two or three times, and bathed his head with cold water, which in a great measure restored the consistency of his ideas. He felt a little sore, but he soon became as chipper and as cheerful as an early robin. His first thought was, that he had escaped being murdered, and he was devoutly thankful to God for the mercy which had again spared his life.

The doctor, after giving him some directions in regard to his head, and the black and blue spots on his body, left the room. He was a naval surgeon, a guest in the hotel, and promised to see his patient again in the morning.

"How do you feel, Somers?" asked Lieutenant Pillgrim, who sat on the bed, gazing with interest, not unmixed with anxiety, at his companion.

"I feel pretty well, considering the hard rap I got on the head."

"You have a hard head, Somers."

"Why so?"

"If you had not, you would have been a dead man. The fellow pounded you with his fist, which is about as heavy as an anvil, and kicked you with his boots, which are large enough and stout enough to make two very respectable gunboats."

"Things are rather mixed in my mind," added Somers, rubbing his head again, as if to explain how a strong-minded young man like himself should be troubled in his upper works.

"I am not surprised at that. You have remained insensible more than half an hour. I was afraid, before the surgeon saw you, that your pipe was out, and you had become a D. D. without taking orders."

"I think I had a narrow escape. What a tiger the fellow was that pitched into me!"

"It was all a mistake on his part."

"Perhaps it was; but that don't make my head feel any better. Who is he, and what is he?"

"He is the captain of a coaster. He had considerable money in his pocket, and he thought you had concealed yourself in his room for the purpose of robbing him. When he saw that you were an officer in the navy, he was overwhelmed with confusion, and really felt very bad about it."

"I don't know that I blame him for what he did, under the circumstances. His conclusion was not a very unnatural one. I don't exactly comprehend how I happen to be in the Continental House, after these stunning events."

"Don't you?" said Pillgrim, with a smile.

"If I had been in condition to expect anything, I should naturally have expected to find myself, on coming to my senses, in the low groggery where I received the blows."

"That is very easily accounted for. I happened to be at the house when you were struck down. I was in the lower room, and heard the row. With others I went up to see what the matter was. I had a carriage in the street, and when I recognized you, the captain of the coaster, at my request, took you up in his arms like a baby, carried you down into the street, and put you into the vehicle, and you were brought here. I presume this will fill up the entire gap in your recollection."

"It is all as clear as mud now," laughed Somers. "Mr. Pillgrim, I am very grateful to you for the kind offices you rendered me."

"Don't mention it, my dear fellow. I should have been worse than a brute if I had done any less than I did."

"That may be; but my gratitude is none the less earnest on that account. Those are villanous people in that house, and I might have been butchered and cut up, if I had been left there."

"I think not. The captain of the coaster is evidently an honest man; at any rate he is very sorry for what he did. But, Somers, my dear fellow, — you will pardon me if I seem impertinent. — how did you happen to be in such a place?" continued Mr. Pillgrim, with a certain affectation of slyness in his look, as though he had caught the exemplary young man in a house where he would not have been willing to be seen.

"How did *you* happen to be there?" demanded Somers.

"I don't profess to be a very proper person. I take my whiskey when I want it."

"So do I; and the only difference between us is, that I never happen to want it."

"I did not go into that house for my whiskey, though. It is rather strange that we should both happen into such a place at the same time."

"Rather strange."

"But I will tell you why I was there," added Pillgrim. "I received a letter from a wounded sailor, asking me to call upon him, and assist him in obtaining a pension."

"Did you, indeed!" exclaimed Somers, amazed at this explanation. "You have also told how I happened to be there."

"How was that?"

"I received just such a letter as that you describe," replied Somers, taking the dirty epistle from his pocket, which he opened and exhibited to his brother officer.

"The handwriting is the same, and the substance of both letters is essentially the same. That's odd — isn't it?" continued the lieutenant, as he drew the epistle he had received from his pocket. "I got mine when I came in, about ten o'clock; and thinking I might go to New York in the morning for a couple of days, I thought I would attend to the matter at once."

Somers took the letters, and compared them. They were written by the same person, on the same kind of paper, and were both mailed on the same day.

"This looks rather suspicious to me," added Pillgrim, reflecting on the circumstances.

"Why suspicious?"

"Why should both of us have been called? Tom Barron claims to have served with me, as he did with you. I don't remember any such person."

"Neither do I."

"Did you find out whether there was any such person at the house as Tom Barron?"

"The woman at the bar told me there was a wounded sailor there whose description answered to that contained in the letter."

"So she told me. Did you see him?"

"No."

"I did not; and between you and me, I don't believe there is any Tom Barron there, or anywhere else. This business must be investigated," said Pillgrim, very decidedly.

Somers did not wish it to be investigated. He was utterly opposed to an investigation, for he was fearful, if the matter should be "ventilated," that more would be shown than he was willing to have exhibited at the present time; in other words, Coles would find out that his enterprising scheme had been exposed to a third person.

"I don't care to be mixed up in any revelations of low life, Mr. Pillgrim; and, as I have lost nothing, and the hard knocks I received were given under a mistake, I think I would rather let the matter rest just where it is."

"Very natural for a young man of your style,' laughed the lieutenant. "You are afraid the people of Pinchbrook will read in the papers that Mr. Somers has been in bad places."

"They might put a wrong construction on the case," replied Somers, willing to have his reasons for avoiding an investigation as strong as possible.

"I can hand these letters over to the police, and let the officers inquire into the matter," added Pillgrim. "They need not call any names."

"I would rather not stir up the dirty pool. Besides, Tom Barron and his mother may be in the house, after all. There is no evidence to the contrary.

"I shall satisfy myself on that point by another visit to the house. If I find there is such a person there, I shall be satisfied."

"That will be the better way."

Just then it occurred to Somers that Coles might have seen him while he was insensible, and was already aware that his scheme had miscarried. He questioned Pillgrim, therefore, in regard to the persons in the bar-room when he entered. From the answers received he satis fied himself that the conspirators had departed before the "row" in the front room occurred.

"Now, Somers, I am going down to that house again before I sleep," said the lieutenant. "This time, I shall take my revolver. Will you go with me?"

"I don't feel exactly able to go out again to-night. My head doesn't feel just right," replied Somers, who, however, had other reasons for keeping his room, the principal of which was the fear that he might meet Coles there, and that, by some accident, his presence in the front room during the conference might be disclosed.

"I think you are right, Somers. You had better keep still to-night," said Pillgrim. "Shall I send you up anything?"

"Thank you; I don't need anything."

"A glass of Bourbon whiskey would do you good. It would quiet your nerves, and put you to sleep."

"Perhaps it would, but I shall lie awake on those terms."

"Don't be bigoted, my dear fellow. Of course I prescribe the whiskey as a medicine."

"You are no surgeon."

"It would quiet your nerves."

"Let them kick, if nothing but whiskey will quiet them," laughed Somers. "Seriously, Mr. Pillgrim, I am very much obliged to you for your kindness, and for your interest in me; but I think I shall be better without the whiskey than with it."

"As you please, Somers. If you are up when I return, I will tell you what I find at the house."

"Thank you; I will leave my door unfastened."

Mr. Pillgrim left the room to make his perilous examination of the locality of his friend's misfortunes. Somers walked the apartment, nervous and excited, considering the events of the evening. He then seated himself, and carefully wrote out the statement of Coles in regard to the Ben Nevis, and the method by which he purposed to operate in getting her to sea as a Confederate cruiser, with extended memoranda of all the conversation to which he had listened. Before he had finished this task, Lieutenant Pillgrim returned.

"It is all right," said he, as he entered the room.

"What's all right?"

"There is such a person as Thomas Barron. The facts contained in the letters are essentially true."

"Then no investigation is necessary," replied Somers, with a feeling of relief.

"None whatever; to-morrow I will see that the poor fellow is sent to the hospital, and his mother provided for."

Mr. Pillgrim, after again recommending a glass of whiskey, took his leave, and Somers finished his paper. He went to bed, and in spite of the fact that he had drank no whiskey, his nerves were quiet; and he dropped asleep like a good Christian, with a prayer in his heart for the "loved ones at home" and elsewhere.

The next morning, though he was still quite sore, and his head felt heavier than usual, he was in much better condition, physically, than could have been expected. After breakfast, as he sat in the parlor of the hotel, he was accosted by a gentleman in blue clothes, with a very small cap on his head.

"An officer of the navy, I perceive," said the stranger, courteously.

"How are you, Langdon?" was the thought, but not the reply, of Somers.

6*

CHAPTER VI.

LIEUTENANT WYNKOOP, R. N.

THE gentlemanly individual who addressed Somers wore the uniform of an English naval officer. By easy and gentle approaches, he proceeded to make himself very agreeable. He was lavish in his praise of the achievements of the "American navy," and was sure that no nation on the face of the globe had ever displayed such skill and energy in creating a war marine. Somers listened patiently to this eloquent and just tribute to the enterprise of his country; and if he had not suspected that the enthusiastic speaker was playing an assumed character, he would have ventured to suggest that the position of John Bull was rather equivocal; that a little less admiration, and a little more genuine sympathy, would be more acceptable.

"We sailors belong to the same fraternity all over the world," said the pretended Englishman. "There is something in sailors which draws them together. I never meet one without desiring to know him better. Allow me to present you my card, and beg the favor of yours in return."

He handed his card to Somers, who read upon it the name of "Lieutenant Wynkoop, R. N." It was elaborately engraved, and our officer began to have some doubts in regard to his new-found acquaintance, for the card could hardly have been got up since the interview of the preceding evening. This gentleman might not be Langdon, after all; but whether he was or not, it was proper to treat him with respect and consideration. Somers wrote his name on a blank card, and gave it to him.

"Thank you, Mr. Somers: here is my hand," said Lieutenant Wynkoop, when he had read the name. "I am happy to make your acquaintance."

Somers took the offered hand, and made a courteous reply, to the salutations of the other.

"May I beg the favor of your company to dinner with me in my private parlor to-day?" continued Mr. Wynkoop. "I have a couple of bottles of fine old sherry, which have twice made the voyage to India, sent to me by an esteemed American friend residing in this city."

"Thank you, Mr. Wynkoop. To the dinner I have not the slightest objection; to the wine I have; and I'm afraid you must reserve it for some one who will appreciate it more highly than I can. I never drink wine."

"Ah, indeed?" said the presumed representative of the royal navy, as he adjusted an eye-glass to his left eye, keeping it in position by contracting the muscles above and below the visual member, which gave a peculiar squint to his expression, very trying to the risibles of his auditor.

"I should be happy to dine with you, but I don't drink wine," repeated Somers, in good-natured but rather bluff tones, for he did not wish to be understood as apologizing for his total abstinence principles.

"I should be glad to meet you in my private parlor, say, at four o'clock, whether you drink wine or not, Mr. Somers."

"Four o'clock?"

"It's rar-ther early, I know. If you prefer five, say the word," drawled Mr. Wynkoop.

"I should say that would be nearer supper time than four," replied Somers, who had lately been in the habit of dining at twelve in Pinchbrook.

"Earlier if you please, then."

"Any hour that is convenient for you will suit me."

"Let it be four, then. But I must acknowledge, Mr. Somers, I am not entirely unselfish in desiring to make your acquaintance. The operations of the American navy have astonished me, and I wish to know more about it. I landed in New York only a few days since, and I improve every opportunity to make the acquaintance of American naval officers. I have not yet visited one of your dock yards."

"I am going over to look at my ship this forenoon, and I should be delighted with your company."

"Thank you! thank you!" exclaimed Mr. Wynkoop. "I shall be under great obligations to you for the favor."

They went to the navy yard, visited the Chatauqua, and other vessels of war fitting out there. Mr. Wynkoop asked a thousand questions about ships, engines, and armaments; and one could hardly help regarding him as the most enthusiastic admirer of naval architecture. Though the gentleman spoke in affected tones, Somers had recognized the voice of Langdon. This was the person, without a doubt, who was to lure him into the Confederate navy, who was to crown his aspirations with a commander's commission, and reward his infidelity with the command of a fine steamer.

Somers was very impatient for the inquiring member of the royal navy to make his proposition; for, strange as it may seem to the loyal reader, he had fully resolved to accept the brilliant offers he expected to receive; to permit Coles to place the name of "John Somers" in the blank of the commander's commission which he had in his possession; and even to take his place on the quarter deck of the Ben Nevis, if it became necessary to carry proceedings to that extent.

But Lieutenant Wynkoop did not even allude to the Confederate navy, or to the Ben Nevis, and did not even attempt to sound the loyalty of his companion. Somers concluded at last that this matter was reserved for the after-dinner conversation; and as he could afford to wait, he continued to give his friend every facility for prosecuting his inquiries into the secret of the marvellous success of the "American navy."

After writing out his statement of Coles's plans, he had carefully and prayerfully considered his duty in relation to the startling information he had thus accidentally obtained. Of course he had no doubt as to what he should do. He must be sure that the Ben Nevis was handed over to the government; that Coles and Langdon were put in close quarters. He only inquired how this should be done. Though the Snowden and the Theban had been captured in the former instance, both Kennedy and Coles had escaped punishment, and one of them was again engaged in the work of pulling down the government.

If he gave information at the present stage of the conspiracy, his plans might be defeated. Though Coles had mentioned no names, it was more than probable that he was aided and abetted in his treasonable projects by other persons. There were traitors in Boston, New York, and Philadelphia, men of wealth and influence, occupying high positions in society, who were engaged in just such enterprises as that which had been revealed to the young naval officer.

Somers felt, therefore, that a premature exposure might ruin himself without overthrowing the conspirators. A word from one of these influential men might lay him on the shelf, to say the least, and remove all suspicion from the guilty ones. He must proceed with the utmost caution, both for his own safety and the success of his enterprise.

Besides, he felt that, if he could get "inside of the ring," he should find out who the great men were that were striking at the heart of the nation in the dark. By obtaining the confidence of the conspirators, he could the more easily baffle them, and do the country a greater service than he could render on the quarter deck of the Chatauqua.

After an earnest and careful consideration of the whole matter, he concluded that his present duty was to pay out rope enough to permit Coles and his guilty associates to hang themselves. For this purpose, he was prepared to receive Langdon with open arms, to accept the commission intended for him, and to enter into the secret councils of his country's bitterest enemies.

Somers, pure and patriotic in his motives, did not for a moment consider that he exposed himself to any risk in thus entering the councils of the wicked, or even in taking a commission in the service of the enemy. He did not intend to aid or abet in the treason of the traitors, and he did not think what might be the result if a rebel commission were found upon his person. He might be killed in battle with this damning document in his pocket. If any of the conspirators were caught, they might denounce him as one of their number. He did not think of these things. He was ambitious to serve his treason-ridden country, and he forgot all about himself.

It was half past three when Somers and Wynkoop returned to the hotel from their visit to the navy yard. Langdon had evidently been in England, for he insisted upon calling it a " dock yard." They separated to dress for dinner, as the courtly John Bull expressed it. At four they met again in the private parlor, where an elegant dinner was served, and where Mr. Wynkoop sipped his sherry " which had twice made the voyage to the East Indies," though it probably came from the cellar of the hotel. When the coffee had been brought in, and the waiters had retired, the representative of the royal navy lighted his cigar, and began, in a very moderate way, to express some slight admiration for the skill and prowess of the rebels. Somers helped him along until he became a thorough rebel.

" With all my admiration for the American navy, Mr. Somers, I find there is a great deal of injustice towards the officers, especially the younger ones," continued Mr. Wynkoop, after he had sufficiently indicated his sympathy for the " noble and gallant people who were struggling against such hodds in the South."—The lieutenant occasionally pressed an *h* into use where it was not needed — probably to be entirely consistent with himself.

" That's true ; and I have suffered from it myself," replied Somers, determined that his companion should want no inducement to make his proposition as soon as he was ready.

"I don't doubt it, Mr. Somers;" and Mr. Wynkoop stated some instances which had come to his knowledge.

Somers then gave a list of his own imaginary grievances, and professed to be greatly dissatisfied with his present position and prospects.

"I think you would do better in the Confederate navy," said the lieutenant, warmly.

"Perhaps I should."

"Whichever side you fight for, you fight for your own country."

"That's true."

"When the South wins, — as win she will, — all who fought against her, will be like prophets in their own country — without honor. In less than two months the independence of the Confederate States will be acknowledged by England and France. I happen to know this."

"It would not surprise me."

"My uncle, the Earl of — never mind; I won't mention his name — my uncle, who is an intimate friend of Palmerston, told me so."

Somers was rather glad to hear it, for it would bring the desolating war to a close. Mr. Wynkoop hesitated no longer. He approached the real business of the meeting rapidly, and in a few moments the commander's commission was on the table. The offer was made, and

Somers, with such apparent qualms of conscience as a naval officer might be expected to exhibit on deserting his flag, accepted the proposition. Mr. Wynkoop went into his sleeping apartment, adjoining the parlor, with the commission in his hand.

He returned in a moment with the name of "John Somers," filled in the blank space left for that purpose, and handed it to his guest.

Somers shuddered when he saw his name written upon such an infernal document; for though he was still true to God, his country, and himself, the paper had an ugly look. But he regarded it only as evidence against the conspirators, rather than against himself; as a necessary formality to enable him to frustrate the designs of traitors, rather than as a blot against his own name.

"Mr. Somers, I congratulate you. If you could be induced to join me in a glass of this old sherry, we would drink to the success of the Louisiana — for that is to be the name of your craft when you get to sea."

"I thank you, Mr. Wynkoop; you must excuse me."

"As you please. Mr. Somers, though I am an Englishman, and belong to the royal navy, it is hardly necessary for me to say now, that I am in the service of the South. I go with you in the Louisiana, as a passenger. Your first work will be to capture one of the California steamers, which I am to transform into a man-of-war, and call the Texas. She will be under my command."

"I am satisfied."

"By the way, Captain Somers," added Wynkoop, as he took a paper from his pocket, "here is the oath of allegiance to the Confederate States of America, which it will be necessary for you to sign."

This was more than Somers had bargained for, and he would have cut off his right hand, or permitted his head to be severed from his body, rather than put his signature to the detested paper. A cold chill crept through his veins, as he glanced at the sheet on which it was printed, and he was afraid all he had done would fail because he could not do this thing.

Lieutenant Wynkoop brought a pen and ink from his sleeping apartment, and placed it by the side of his guest.

"I would rather not sign this just now," said Somers. "It might get me into trouble."

"Very well; we will attend to that after you get on board of the Ben Nevis," replied Wynkoop, as he took the oath and the commission, with the pen and ink, and went into his chamber again.

He was absent several minutes this time, and Somers had an opportunity to review his position.

"Here is your commission, Captain Somers," said the lieutenant, as he placed the document on the table. "On the whole, I think you had better sign the oath now."

"I think it will do just as well when we get off."

"Perhaps it will; here are your orders," said he.

handing Somers another paper, and placing that containing the oath on the table.

At this moment, Somers heard a step in the direction of the bedroom. He turned, with surprise, to see who it was, for he had heard no one enter.

"Ah, Somers, I am glad to see you," said the new arrival, stepping up to the table, and glancing at the papers which lay open there.

It was Lieutenant Pillgrim.

CHAPTER VII

LANGDON'S LETTERS.

IT had been no part of Somers's purpose to bear the whole responsibility of the transactions in which he had so promptly engaged. Mr. Waldron would return in a few days, and on his arrival, the overburdened young officer intended to confide the momentous secret to him, receiving the benefit of his advice and support in the great business he had undertaken.

After the kind treatment he had received at the hands of Lieutenant Pillgrim, he was rather disposed to make him a confidant; but he knew so little about his travelling companion, that though he had no question about his fidelity and honor, he was not quite willing to stake everything on his judgment and discretion, as he must do, if he opened the subject to him.

Somers was not a little surprised to see Mr. Pillgrim enter the parlor in that unceremonious way. It indicated a degree of intimacy between the two gentleman that gave him an unpleasant impression, which, however, he had no time to follow out to its legitimate issue.

"Excuse me, Mr. Wynkoop," said Lieutenant Pillgrim, as he paused at the side of the table, "for entering in this abrupt manner. I have been knocking at your door for some time, without obtaining a response."

"You went to the wrong door. That's my bedroom."

"So I perceive, now."

"But there is no harm done; on the contrary, I am very glad to see you. Sit down and take a glass of wine with me. Mr. Somers does not indulge."

"Mr. Somers is a very proper young man," said the lieutenant, with a pleasant smile, as he glanced again at the papers which lay open on the table. "I have been looking for you, Somers, but it was only to ask you what the prospect is on board the Chatauqua. I have not been on board to-day."

"I think we shall be wanted by to-morrow or next day," replied Somers, who could not help seeing that the eye of his superior officer was fixed on the commander's commission, which lay open before him.

"Indeed! I am glad to know this, for I had made up my mind to go to New York in the morning. Of course I shall not go."

"Sit down, Mr. — Really, sir, you must excuse me, but I have forgotten your name," said Mr. Wynkoop.

"Lieutenant Pillgrim — at your service. It is not very surprising that you should forget it, since we have met but once; not half so surprising as that I should force myself into your rooms, on so short an acquaintance."

"Don't mention it, my dear fellow. We sailors are brothers all over the world. Sit down, and take a glass of sherry with me. It's a capital wine — made two voyages to India."

"Excuse me, Mr. Wynkoop; I merely called to invite you to spend the evening with me. I have a plan that will use up two or three hours very pleasantly."

"Thank you, Mr. Pillgrim. You are a friend in need, and a friend indeed."

"I see that you and Mr. Somers have business, and I will take my leave."

"I should be happy to have you remain, but if you will not, I will join you in half an hour in the reading-room. Better sit down, and wait here."

"I will not interrupt your business with Mr. Somers," replied Lieutenant Pillgrim, again glancing curiously at the documents on the table.

Greatly to the relief of Somers, his fellow-officer left the room. This visit had been a most unfortunate one, for the lieutenant could not have avoided seeing the nature of the papers on the table. But as Somers was a true and loyal man, his conscience accused him of no wrong, and he had no fears in regard to the result. This revelation simply imposed upon him the necessity of making

Mr. Pillgrim his confidant, which he proposed to do at the first convenient opportunity.

"You think you will not sign the oath to-night, Mr. Somers?" said his companion.

"It had better be deferred," replied Somers, as he folded up the commission, and put it in his pocket, regarding it as the most important evidence in his possession against Coles, and a sufficient confirmation of the truth of the statement he had so carefully written out the night before.

"Suit yourself, Somers. We shall not differ about these small matters," added Wynkoop, as he folded up the oath, and put it in his pocket. "By the way, Somers, what do you think of our friend Pillgrim?"

"He is a fine fellow, and I am told he is a good officer. I was not aware that you knew him."

"I have only met him once, just as I met you. How do you think he stands affected towards our cause?"

"Not well."

"So I feared."

"He is a loyal man, though a Virginian."

"Do you think I could make anything of him?"

"I am satisfied you could not."

"I did not dare to try him. I gave him a chance to nibble at my bait, but he wouldn't bite. Perhaps, when I know him better, he will come round; for I don't think there are many of these Yankee officers that have any real heart in their work."

"You are utterly mistaken," said Somers; but remembering that he was hardly in a position to defend his loyal comrades in the navy, he did not seriously combat the proposition of the rebel emissary.

As the business of the interview was now finished, Somers shook hands with his agreeable host — though his heart repelled the act, — and took leave of him. He hastened to his chamber, agitated and excited by the strange and revolting scene through which he had just passed. It was some time before he was calm enough to think coherently of what he had done, and of the compact he had made. He wished very much to see Mr. Waldron now; indeed, he felt the absolute necessity of confiding to some trustworthy person the momentous secret he had obtained, which burned in his soul like an evil deed.

If Lieutenant Pillgrim had not actually read his commission when it lay on the table, he must, at least, have suspected that all was not right with his shipmate. He must, therefore, confide in him, and without the loss of another moment, he hastened to his room for this purpose; but the lieutenant was not there. He searched for him in all the public rooms of the hotel, but without success. Remembering that his fellow-officer was to meet Mr. Wynkoop in the reading-room half an hour from the time they parted, he waited there over an hour, but the appointment evidently was not kept by either party.

Somers did not wish to sleep another night without sharing his great secret with some one; for if anything should happen to him, he reasoned, the commission and the orders might be found in his possession, and subject him to very unpleasant suspicions, if they did not expose him to the actual charge of complicity with the enemies of his country. He waited in the vicinity of the office till midnight, hoping to see Mr. Pillgrim; but he did not appear, and he reluctantly retired to his chamber.

When he carried his key to the office in the morning, there was a note in his box, addressed to him. The ink of the direction was hardly dry, and the lap of the envelope was still wet where it had been moistened to seal it. Somers opened it. He was surprised and startled at its contents; but the writer had evidently made a mistake in the superscription. It was as follows:—

"My Dear Pillgrim: I have just sent a note to Somers, saying that the Ben Nevis has sailed,— which is a fact,— and that he must join her at Mobile, where she will run in a cargo of arms and provisions. Act accordingly. How is this?

Langdon."

Both the name and the import of the letter implied that the note was not intended for Somers, though it was directed to him. The writer had evidently written two notes, and in his haste had misdirected the envelopes.

"My dear Pillgrim!" The note was intended for his fellow-officer. Was Pillgrim a confederate of Langdon? It looked so, incredible as it seemed.

Somers was bewildered for a moment, but he was too good a strategist to be overwhelmed. Restoring the note to its envelope, he readjusted the lap, which was still wet, and the letter looked as though it had not been opened. He returned it to the box under his key, and perceived that there was also a note in Mr. Pillgrim's box. As soon as the mistake was discovered, the letters would be changed. He returned to his room to await the result.

Somers had made an astounding discovery by the merest accident in the world. Things were not what they seemed. Mr. Pillgrim had relations of some kind with Langdon, *alias* Lieutenant Wynkoop. His entering the parlor while they were at dinner was not so accidental a circumstance as it had appeared. Who and what was Lieutenant Pillgrim? The belief that he had met him somewhere before they came together at Newport, still haunted Somers; but he was in no better condition now than then to solve the mystery.

In half an hour he went down to the office again. The note to Mr. Pillgrim was gone; but there was one for himself in the box. He took it out; the direction was not in the same handwriting as before. **Mr Pillgrim** had probably discovered the mistake, and changed the letters, without a suspicion that the one addressed to himself had been read. Somers opened the note, which contained the information he expected to find there in regard to the Ben Nevis, and was signed by Wynkoop.

Beyond the possibility of a doubt now, Lieutenant Pillgrim was a confederate of Langdon. Of course, he knew Coles. He was a Virginian, and it was now certain to Somers, if to no one else, that his loyalty had been justly suspected. He had doubtless entered the navy again for a purpose. What that purpose was, remained yet to be exposed. From the depths of his heart, Somers thanked God that this discovery had been made; and he determined to put it to good use. He was now more anxious than before to meet his friend Mr. Waldron, and communicate the startling information to him.

From the morning papers he saw that the Ben Nevis, whose name had been changed to that of a famous Union general, had actually sailed, as Langdon's note informed him. In the forenoon, he went to the navy yard, expecting to find the ship ready to go into commission; but he learned that the bed-plates of her pivot guns had to be recast, and that she would not be ready for another week. He also learned that his friend Mr. Waldron had been taken down with typhoid fever at his home, and was then in a critical condition.

Somers was not only shocked, but disconcerted by this intelligence, for it deprived him of the friend and counsellor whom he needed in this emergency. After careful deliberation, he obtained a furlough of a week, and went to the home of Mr. Waldron; but the sufferer could not even be seen, much less consulted on a matter of business. Left to act for himself, he hastened to New York, and then to Boston, to ascertain what he could in regard to the Ben Nevis. So far as he could learn, everything was all right in regard to her. After a short visit to Pinchbrook, he hastened back to Philadelphia, and found the Chatauqua hauled out into the stream, and ready to go into commission at once. Lieutenant Pillgrim and the other officers had already gone on board. Under these circumstances, Somers had not a moment to see Langdon. He took possession of his state-room, and at once had all the work he could do, in the discharge of his duty.

At meridian the ensign was run up, and the ship went into commission under the command of Captain Cascabel. Mr. Pillgrim was doing duty as executive officer, though a substitute for Mr. Waldron was expected before the ship sailed. Somers was uneasy, and dissatisfied with himself. He began to feel that he had left a duty unperformed. He had intended to expose the conspiracy before the Chatauqua sailed, and thus relieve himself from the heavy responsibility that rested upon him. Yet to whom could he speak? Mr. Waldron was still dangerously ill. Mr. Pillgrim was evidently a traitor himself.

He could give his information to the United States marshal at Philadelphia; but how could he prove his allegations? Langdon and Coles he had not seen since his return, and perhaps they were in another part of the country by this time. He had the commander's commission and the written orders, but in the absence of the principals, he feared these would be better evidence against himself than against the conspirators.

The Ben Nevis had sailed, and the worst she could do at present would be to run the blockade. The Chautauqua was generally understood to be ordered to Mobile, where the Ben Nevis was to run in, and fit out for her piratical cruise. After a great deal of serious reflection, Somers came to the unsatisfactory conclusion that he must keep his secret. He could not denounce Mr. Pillgrim as a rebel, with his present information, without exposing himself to greater peril than the real criminal. Besides, he was to be with the lieutenant, and he was going to Mobile. He could watch the traitor, and await the appearance of the Ben Nevis, when she arrived at the station.

Somers was not satisfied with this conclusion, but his judgment assured him his intended course of action was the best the circumstances would admit. Thus settling the question, he attended to his duty with his usual zeal and energy.

CHAPTER VIII.

THE UNITED STATES STEAMER CHATAUQUA.

SOMERS had served in several vessels, but never before had he gone on board his ship with a heavier responsibility resting upon him, than when he took his station on the deck of the Chatauqua. He was now a ward-room officer, and as such he would be required to keep a watch, and be in command of the deck. But in addition to his professional duties, he had in his keeping valuable but dangerous information, of which he must make a judicious use.

The young officer was perfectly familiar with the routine of his duties. He knew the ship from stem to stern, and from keel to truck. He felt entirely at home, therefore, and hoped soon to merit the approbation of his superiors. He was formally presented to Captain Cascabel and the other officers of the ship. He was kindly and cordially greeted by all. Mr. Pillgrim, as acting first lieutenant, proceeded at once to make out the watch, quarter, and station bill; and, whatever his political principles, it must be confessed that he performed this difficult duty with skill and judgment.

Every day, until the ship sailed, the crew were exercised at the guns, and in all the evolutions required for carrying on ship's duty, from "fire stations" to piping down the hammocks. They made the usual proficiency, and were soon in condition to work together — to handle the ship in a tornado, or to meet an enemy. On the fourth day, when Mr. Pillgrim was superseded by Mr. Hackleford, who was appointed in the place of Mr. Waldron, everything was in an advanced stage of progress.

The Chatauqua was a screw steam sloop of war, of the first class. She carried ten guns, and was about fourteen hundred tons burden. Her complement of officers and men was about two hundred and fifty, including forty-two attached to the engineer's department. The ship was a two-decker. On the upper or spar deck was placed her armament, consisting of two immense pivot guns and eight broadside guns.

Below this was the berth deck, on which all the officers and men ate and slept. The after part was appropriated to the officers, and the forward part to the men. The former were provided with cabins and state-rooms, while the latter swung their hammocks to the deck beams over their heads.

As most of our readers have probably never seen the interior of a ship of war, we present on the adjoining page a plan of that portion of the vessel occupied by the officers. The round part is the stern of the ship, and the diagram includes a little less than one third of the whole length of the vessel.

A. The Captain's cabin, to which are attached the six small apartments on each side of it.

1. The Companion-way, or stairs, by which the cabin is reached from the deck.

2, 3. Store-rooms.

4. Water-closet.

5. Pantry.

6, 7. State-rooms.

B. The Ward-room, in which there is a table, long enough to accommodate the eight officers who occupy this apartment.

8. First Lieutenant's state-room.
9. Second " " "
10. Third " " "
11. Fourth " " "
12. Chief Engineer's " "
13. Master's " "
14. Paymaster's " "
15. Surgeon's " "
16. First Assistant Engineers' state-room.
17. Second Assistant Engineers' room.

C. The Steerage, occupied by Midshipmen and Masters' Mates.

D. Third Assistant Engineer's room.

18. The Armory.

19. Ward-room pantry, through which passes the mizzen-mast.

20, 20. Berths.

21, 21. Mess store-rooms.

In the floor of the ward-room, between the state-room, 7 and 12, there are two scuttles leading down to the magazine, so that, during an action, all the powder is passed up through this room. Woollen screens are hung up on each side of these scuttles, when they are opened, to prevent any spark from being carried down to the powder.

There are four other scuttles leading down into the hold from the ward-room to the various store-rooms located there, and several in the floor abreast of the steerage.

On the forward part of the berth deck, just abaft the foremast, there are four state-rooms for the use of the carpenter, gunner, boatswain, and sailmaker. All persons except those mentioned sleep in hammocks.

The engine department of the Chatauqua consisted of one chief, two first assistant, two second assistant, and one third assistant engineers, with eighteen firemen and eighteen coal heavers. The chief engineer is a ward-room officer. He has the sole charge of the engine, and all persons connected with its management, but he keeps no watch. The other engineers obey the orders of their chief, and are divided into watches. They attend to the actual working of the engine. The firemen are also classified, and receive different grades of pay, a portion of them attending to the oiling of the machinery, — called "oilers," — while others superintend or feed the fires, and do other work connected with the engine and boilers. The coal-heavers convey the fuel from the coal bunkers to the furnaces.

Mr. Ensign Somers was the fourth lieutenant of the Chatauqua, and occupied the last state-room on the left, as you enter the ward-room. It was a nice little apartment, and the young officer was as happy as a lord when he was fully installed in his new quarters. And well might one who had commenced his naval career as an ordinary seaman, sleeping in a hammock, and who had never before known anything better than the confined accommodations of the steerage, have been delighted with his present comfortable and commodious quarters.

His state-room was lighted by a bull's eye, or round glass window, which could be opened in port, or in pleasant weather at sea. The room contained but one berth, which was quite wide for a ship, supplied with an excellent mattress; and one who could not sleep well in such a bed must be troubled with a rebellious conscience. There was also a bureau, the upper drawer of which, when the front was dropped down, became a convenient writing desk, supplied with small drawers, shelves, and pigeon-holes. The room was carpeted, and contained all that a reasonable man could require to make him comfortable and happy.

There was only one drawback upon the happiness of Somers; and that was the absence of Mr. Waldron. There was not one among the officers whom he could now call by the endearing name of friend, though all of them were good officers and gentlemanly men, and he had no reason to anticipate any difficulty with any of them, unless it was with Mr. Pillgrim. He sighed for the friendly guidance and the genial companionship of the late commander of the Rosalie, especially in view of the embarrassing circumstances which surrounded him.

But it was some compensation to know that his old shipmate, Tom Longstone, had been promoted to the rank of boatswain, and ordered to the Chatauqua. The old man's splendid behavior in Doboy Sound had enabled Mr. Waldron to secure this favor for him, and to obtain his appointment to his own ship. Mr. Longstone, as he must hereafter be called, came on board in a uniform of bright blue, and his dress so altered his appearance that Somers hardly recognized him. The old salt had always been very careful about "putting on airs," when he was a common sailor or a petty officer; but he knew how to be a gentleman, and his new dignity sat as easily upon him as though he had been brought up in the ward-room. Though he looked well, and carried himself like an officer, he could not immediately adapt his language to his new position. He was a representative sailor, and he could not help being "salt."

The boatswain was Somers's only real friend on board, and the distance between a ward-room officer and a forward officer was so great that he was not likely to realize any especial satisfaction from the friendship; but it was pleasant to know that there was even one in the ship who was devoted to him, heart and soul.

"All hands, up anchor!" piped the boatswain; and it was a pleasant sound to the fourth lieutenant of the Chatauqua, as doubtless it was to all hands, for "lying in the stream" is stupid work to an expectant crew.

The ship got under way with all the order and regularity which prevail on board a man-of-war, and in a short time was standing down the Delaware River. Her great guns pealed the customary salute, and as the wind was fair, her top-sails and top-gallant-sails were shaken out as soon as she had passed from the narrow river into the broad bay. Off the capes the sealed orders were opened; and it proved, as the knowing ones had anticipated, that the Chatauqua was bound to the blockading station off Mobile Bay.

At eight o'clock in the evening the ship was out of sight of land. Everything on board was in regular sea trim. Mr. Garboard, the third lieutenant, had the deck, and the other officers were in the ward-room, or in their state-rooms. They were discussing the merits of the ship, or the probable work before them at Mobile; for a great naval attack in that quarter was confidently predicted. The "Old Salamander," "Brave Old Salt," as Admiral Farragut was familiarly called, was understood to be making preparations for one of his tremendous onslaughts.

Somers was occupied in his state-room, putting his books, papers, and clothing in order, which he had not had time to do before to his satisfaction. He placed his Testament on the bureau, where it could be taken up for a moment without delay, and where it would constantly remind him of his duty, and of the loved ones at home, with whom the precious volume seemed to be inseparably associated.

Among his papers were the rebel commission, the written orders, and the statement he had made of the interview between Coles and Langdon, which had been extended so as to contain a full account of his conference with "Mr. Wynkoop," and his inquiries into the character of the Ben Nevis, in Boston and New York. These documents brought forcibly to his mind his relations with Lieutenant Pillgrim, who was still a mystery to him. Since Somers had come on board of the Chatauqua, not a syllable had been breathed about the dinner with the "officer of the royal navy." As Mr. Pillgrim doubtless believed he had changed the letters, and thus corrected his confederate's mistake, before the letter intended for him had fallen into Somers's hand, the lieutenant had no reason to suppose his treasonable position was even suspected.

Somers felt that he had a battle to fight with Mr. Pillgrim, and the suspense was intolerable, not to mention the hypocrisy and deceit which this double character required of him. Now, more than before, he regretted the absence of Mr. Waldron, who would have been a rock of safety and strength to him in the trials that beset him. While he was moodily overhauling his papers, and thinking of his difficult situation, Mr. Pillgrim knocked at the door of his room, and was invited to enter.

"Ah, making stowage, are you, Somers?" said the lieutenant, pleasantly.

"Yes, sir; putting things to rights a little."

"It's a good plan to have everything in its place," added Pillgrim, as he took up the little Testament which lay on the bureau. "You are a good boy, I see, and read the book."

"That was given me by my mother, and I value it very highly."

"Then I shouldn't think you would want to wear it out."

"She gave it to me to use, and I am afraid, if she saw it was not soiled by handling, she would think it had not been well used."

"I am glad you use it. I don't fail to read mine morning and evening."

Somers could not believe him, and he could not see that a traitor to his country should have any use for the New Testament.

"By the way, Somers, did you see your friend Wynkoop again before we sailed?" added Mr. Pillgrim.

"I did not; I have not seen him since we dined together. I judge that you were better acquainted with him than I was."

"My acquaintance with him was very slight. By the papers I saw on the table before you, when you were at dinner, I think you made good use of the short time you knew each other."

"To what do you allude?" asked Somers, now assured that Mr. Pillgrim knew the nature of the papers.

"To your commission as a commander in the Confederate navy. Mr. Somers, I could not believe my eyes."

"Were you very much astonished?"

"If I had been told that President Lincoln had gone over to the rebels, I should not have been more astonished. Your conduct has severely embarrassed me. It was my duty to denounce you as a traitor, in the service of the enemy, but — "

At that instant the rattle of the drum, beating to quarters, caused both of them to hurry on deck.

CHAPTER IX.

IN THE STATE-ROOM.

SOMERS took his station on the quarter deck, near the mizzen-mast, while Mr. Pillgrim went forward to the forecastle. The guns were cast loose, and the crew exercised at quarters for a few moments, just as though there were an enemy's ship near. This manœuvre was executed for the purpose of perfecting the officers and crew in discipline; and it is not an uncommon thing to turn up all hands in the dead of the night for this object, for it is easier to correct mistakes at such times than when in the presence of the enemy. As there was no Confederate ship in sight, all hands were presently piped below, and Somers returned to his state-room, where he was soon joined by Mr. Pillgrim, who evidently wished to prolong the conversation which had been commenced before the ship beat to quarters.

"Mr. Somers, you and I have been friends for some little time," the lieutenant began, "and I confess that I have been deeply interested in you, not only on your own account, but for the sake of our friends at Newport."

"Thank you, Mr. Pillgrim," said Somers, as the gentleman paused. "I am greatly obliged to you, and I hope I shall always merit your good opinion."

"I'm afraid not, my young friend; at least, you have not commenced this cruise very well, having first sold yourself to the enemy."

"Do you think I have done that, Mr. Pillgrim?" demanded Somers, not a little excited by the charge, from such a source.

"I know you have. I saw your commission on the table."

"I took the commission, I grant, but I have no intention of using it."

"Why did you take it then?"

"For the purpose of gaining information."

"Have you gained it?" demanded Mr. Pillgrim, with a hardly perceptible sneer.

"I have."

"You received written orders, also."

"I did; and if I had obtained a foothold on the deck of the vessel to which I was ordered, you would have seen how quick I should have passed her over to my government."

"That is a very plausible explanation, Mr. Somers," added the lieutenant. "But why did you sign the oath of allegiance to the Southern Confederacy?"

"I did not."

"I beg your pardon, but I saw the document with your signature affixed to it."

"You are mistaken, Mr. Pillgrim."

"Can I refuse to believe the evidence of my own eyes?"

"Nevertheless, I must persist in saying that I did not sign the oath."

"After what you have done, Mr. Somers, I could hardly expect you to acknowledge it to a loyal officer. Are you aware that any court martial would convict you, on the evidence against you, of treason, and sentence you to death?"

"I think not, when it was made to appear that all I did was in the service of my country."

Somers shuddered when he thought of a traitor's doom, and for the first time realized that he had accumulated more evidence against himself than against the conspirators. The commander's commission and the written orders were almost, if not quite, enough to hang him.

"You don't believe what you say, Mr. Somers, and of course you cannot expect me to believe it," said Pillgrim, when he saw his brother officer musing, and looking rather anxious.

"I speak the truth, Mr. Pillgrim," replied Somers, unable to turn his attention entirely away from the consequences which might follow some of these appearances against him.

"Somers, I have felt a deep interest in you. I have all along desired to be your friend. This is the only reason why I did not prefer charges against you before the ship sailed. Now, I advise you not to deny what is as plain as truth can make it. I am your friend. Own up to me, and I promise never to betray you."

"Would your friend Langdon, *alias* Lieutenant Wynkoop, R. N., be equally considerate?" asked Somers, provoked into making this unguarded remark by the hypocrisy of Pillgrim.

If the second lieutenant of the Chatauqua had received the bolt from a thunder cloud he could not have been more astonished. He started back, turned pale, and quivered with emotion.

"Who?" demanded he, with a tremendous effort to recover his self-possession.

"Do you think, Mr. Pillgrim, that I am a little lamb, that can be led round with a silken string?" replied Somers, with energy. "You are my superior officer, and as such I will respect and obey you until — until — "

"Until what?"

"Until the day of reckoning comes. When you stand up in my presence and charge me with being a traitor to my country, you had better remember that such charges, like chickens, will go home to roost."

"I was not brought up in a barn yard, Mr. Somers, and such comparisons are beyond my comprehension."

"Wherever you were brought up, I think my language is plain enough to be understood by a person of your intelligence."

Perhaps it was fortunate for both parties that a knock at the state-room door disturbed the conference at this exciting moment. Somers opened the door.

"Mr. Hackleford desires to see Mr. Somers on deck," said a midshipman.

"Excuse me for a few moments, Mr. Pillgrim," said Somers, as he closed his desk and locked it.

"Certainly, sir; but I should be happy to see you when you are disengaged. I will remain here if you please."

"I will join you as soon as I can."

It was warm below, and both Pillgrim and Somers had thrown off their coats, and laid them on the bed. Somers slipped on his own, as he supposed, and hastened on deck to meet the first lieutenant. The garment seemed rather large for him, and there were several papers in the breast pocket which did not belong to him. Then he was aware that he had taken the second lieutenant's coat instead of his own.

Mr. Hackleford wished to obtain some information from him in regard to one of the petty officers, and when Somers had answered the questions he went below again. The papers in the pocket of Pillgrim's coat seemed to burn his fingers when he touched them. The owner was a traitor, and perhaps these documents might contain valuable intelligence. Under ordinary circumstances it would have been the height of perfidy to look at one of them; but, in the present instance, he felt justified in glancing at them. The state-room of the second assistant engineers was open and lighted, but neither of these officers was there. Stepping into the room, he opened the papers and glanced at their contents. Only one of them contained anything of importance. This was a note from a person who signed himself simply " Irvine," but it was in the handwriting of Langdon. The only clause in the epistle that was intelligible to Somers was this: " Have just heard from B——. The Ben Nevis, he says, will make Wilmington after leaving St. John. Plenty of guns there. She will sail July 4."

Whether " B——" meant Boston or some person's name, Somers could not determine; but the fact in regard to the Ben Nevis was of the utmost consequence. Hastily folding up the note, he returned the package of papers to the pocket where he had found them. Taking off the coat as he entered the ward-room, he went into the state-room, where Mr. Pillgrim was still waiting for him, with the garment on his arm. He threw it upon the bed as he entered, and his companion was not even aware of the mistake which had been made.

" Mr. Somers, you were making some grave charges against me when you were called away," said the lieutenant.

"Not half so grave as those you made against me," replied Somers.

"Those can be proved."

"I made no charges. I only mentioned the name of your friend Langdon."

"I don't know him," added Pillgrim, doggedly.

"I beg your pardon, as you did mine, just now."

"Which means that you doubt my word."

"As you did mine."

"Somers, I am not to be trifled with," said Pillgrim, sternly.

"Neither am I."

"Be cautious, or I will denounce you to the captain at once," added the lieutenant, in low and threatening tones.

"Proceed, and then I shall be at liberty to take the next step."

"What's that?"

"Do you think I intend to show you my hand?" said Somers, with a meaning smile.

Pillgrim bit his lip with vexation. He seemed to be completely cornered. He evidently believed that his companion knew more than "the law allows."

"Mr. Pillgrim, I am no traitor; you know this as well as I do. Whatever papers I took from your friend Langdon, alias Wynkoop, were taken with a view to serve my country."

"You signed the oath of allegiance he offered you."

"It is false!" replied Somers, angrily.

"Be calm, Mr. Somers. I am no hypocrite, as you are," added Pillgrim. "I have heard that you have a talent for overhearing other people's conversation."

"In the service of my country I am willing to do even this," said Somers, indignantly.

"No matter about that. You have hinted that I am a traitor."

"If the hint is not sufficient, I declare that such is the fact."

Somers was roused to a high pitch of excitement, and he was not as prudent as he was wont to be. He was not playing a part now; he was talking and acting as he wanted to talk and act. He was calling treason and treachery by their right names.

"Explain, Mr. Somers," said Pillgrim, who grew cooler as his companion became hotter.

"You are in league with the enemies of your country. You and others have just started a steamer for St. John, which you intend to fit out as a Confederate cruiser — the Ben Nevis, of which you and your fellow-conspirators did me the honor to give me the command."

Pillgrim smiled blandly.

"And you accepted the command?"

"For a purpose, I did."

"You have not explained why you connect me with this affair. You spoke of some one whom you call Langdon. I don't know him."

"You — do!"

"Prove it."

"He addresses a note to you, calling you 'my dear Pillgrim,' and signs himself, familiarly, 'Langdon.'"

"Then you have been reading my letters — have you?"

"It was addressed to me, and put in my box at the hotel."

The second lieutenant turned pale, then red. He walked up and down the state-room several times in silence. He could not deny the fact alleged. While he walked, Somers explained how he had read the note, and then put it back in the box. Pillgrim understood it.

"Of course you know Coles," continued Somers placing a heavy emphasis on the name of this worthy.

The lieutenant halted before his companion, and looked earnestly and inquiringly into his face. Somers returned his gaze with unflinching resolution. There was a smile upon his face, for he believed that he had thrown a red-hot shot into the enemy.

"Coles!" said Pillgrim.

"Coles!" repeated Somers.

"Mr. Somers, you are a fool!"

"Pray, where were you when human wisdom was distributed?"

"Do you know Coles?" asked Pillgrim.

"I think I should know Coles if I saw him."

"No, you wouldn't."

"He is the greatest villain that ever went unhung."

"Except yourself. Somers, this is child's play. You have made me your enemy, but let us fight it out like men."

"I will do so with pleasure when you take your place on the deck of a rebel vessel, where you belong."

"A truce to child's play, I say again. We must settle this matter here and now."

"It can't be done."

"It must be done, or I will inform Captain Cascabel who and what you are before the first watch is out. Probably he will wish to see your Confederate commission and your letter of instructions."

"When he does, I have something else to show him," replied Somers, whose answer was sufficiently indefinite to make the traitor look very stormy and anxious.

"Can you show him a Confederate oath of allegiance signed by me?"

"No."

"Then he will be more likely to hear me than you," added the lieutenant, whose countenance now looked as malignant as that of a demon. "You have subscribed to that oath; I have not."

"It is false!"

"So you said before."

"Prove it."

"Here," continued Pillgrim, taking from his pocket

the document which had been offered to Somers by Wynkoop.

The young officer glanced at it, and on the line for the signature, he saw, with horror and indignation, the name of "John Somers," apparently in his own handwriting. Undoubtedly it was a forgery, but it was so well done that even the owner of the name could hardly distinguish it from his usual signature.

"It is a forgery," gasped Somers, appalled at the deadly peril which seemed to be in his path.

"Prove it," said the lieutenant, with a mocking smile.

Somers groaned in spirit. It would be impossible for him to prove that the signature was a forgery. Even his best friends would acknowledge it, so well was it executed.

"I have you, Somers," said Pillgrim, exultingly. "Let us understand each other. You are mine, Somers, or you hang! Somers, I am Coles!"

CHAPTER X.

THE CHIEF CONSPIRATOR.

LIEUTENANT PILLGRIM rattled off the sentences in which he acknowledged his complicity with treason with a smile of malignant triumph on his face. He gloated over his victim as the evil one might be supposed to do over a soul wrenched from truth and virtue. He believed that he had Somers in a position where he could not betray him, or even resent his tyranny.

For the first time Somers realized that he had been imprudent in exposing himself to the machinations of these evil men. Before he had only felt a little uncomfortably, and harbored a vague suspicion that, in attempting to overreach others, he had committed himself. He had learned in his babyhood that it is dangerous to play with fire, but had never believed it so fully as at this moment. He had touched the pitch, and felt that he had been defiled by it. Though his conscience kept assuring him he was innocent, and protesting against a harsh judgment, he could not help regretting that he had not exposed the villains before he left Philadelphia, and permitted the consequences to take care of themselves.

But stronger than any other impression, at this eventful moment, was the feeling that he was no match for men so deeply versed in treason and wickedness as Pillgrim and his confederates. He had played at the game of strategy, and been beaten. While he thought he was leading them on to confusion, they were actually entwining the meshes of the net around him.

Mr. Pillgrim had just declared that he was the mysterious Coles. Somers, at first, found it very difficult to realize the fact. He had really seen Coles but once; but they had spent some hours together. At that time Coles wore long, black whiskers, which concealed two thirds of his face; Pillgrim wore no beard, not even a mustache. Coles was dressed in homely garments; Pillgrim, in an elegant uniform. Coles's hair was short and straight; Pillgrim's, long and curly at the ends.

In height, form, and proportions, they were the same; and the difference between Coles and Pillgrim was really nothing which might not have been produced with a razor, a pair of barber's shears, and the contrast of dress. The familiarity of the lieutenant's expression, before unexplained, was now accounted for; and before his tyrant spoke again, Somers was satisfied that he actually stood in the presence of Coles.

Pillgrim stood with folded arms, gazing at his victim,

and enjoying the confusion which Somers could not conceal. The persecutor was a confident man, and fully believed that he was master of the situation, and that Somers would do anything he asked of him, even to going over into the rebel ranks. He was mistaken; for Somers, deep as he felt that he was in hot water, would have chosen to hang at the fore yard-arm, rather than betray his country, or be false to her interests.

"You just now remarked that you should know Coles if you saw him," sneered Pillgrim.

"I know you now," replied Somers, bitterly.

"I see you do; but you will know me better before we part."

"I know you well enough now. You are a rebel and a traitor; and what I said of Coles I say of you, — that you are the greatest villain that ever went unhung."

"I don't like that kind of language, Mr. Somers," replied Pillgrim, with entire coolness and self-possession. "It isn't the kind of language which one gentleman should apply to another."

"Gentleman!" said Somers, with curling lip; "I applied it to a rebel and a traitor."

"In the present instance it is mutiny. I am your superior officer."

"You are out of place; you don't belong here."

"Your place is on the quarter deck of the Ben Nevis; and perhaps it will be when she goes into commission as a Confederate cruiser."

"Never!" exclaimed Somers, with energy.

"My dear Mr. Somers, be prudent. Some of the officers might hear you."

"I don't care if they all hear me."

"You talk and act like a boy, Somers. I beg you to consider that your neck and mine are in the same noose. If I hang, you hang with me."

Somers groaned, for he could not see where his vindication was to come from.

"You seem to understand your situation, and at the same time you appear to be quite willing to throw yourself into the fire. Let me call your attention to the fact that fire will burn."

"Better burn or hang, than be a traitor."

"Be reasonable, Somers. I do not propose to ask anything of you which will compromise your position in the navy; but I repeat, you are mine."

"I don't understand you."

"I have told you my secret. You know that I am in the Confederate service; that I have fitted out a vessel to cruise for Yankee ships. I am willing you should know this, for you dare not violate my confidence."

"Perhaps I dare."

"If you do, you are a dead man."

"Will you kill me?"

"If necessary."

"I have usually been able to defend myself," replied Somers, with dignity.

"I am not an assassin. A court martial will do all I wish done if you are not prudent and devoted, as you should be. The Confederate oath of allegiance signed by you is good testimony."

"I didn't sign it. The signature is a forgery."

"My dear fellow, what possible difference does that make? It is well done — is it not?"

"Perhaps it is. Where did you get it?"

"Langdon gave it to me."

"Did he sign my name to it?"

"Possibly; but even grant that I did it myself — what then?"

"You are a greater villain than I ever gave Coles the credit of being."

"Thank you!"

"Where is Langdon now?"

"In New York — where he can be reached if you make it necessary to convene a court martial."

"Is he a naval officer?"

"Yes; he has been a Confederate agent in London for the past two years. Since the English have become a little particular about letting steamers out for the Confederates, he buys them on this side."

"What do you want of me, Mr. — Pillgrim? if that is your name?"

"That is my name. I don't want much of you."

"What?"

"I am not ready to tell you until you are in a proper frame of mind. You are rather childish to-night. After you have thought the matter over, you will be a man, and be reasonable. Let me see: Garboard has the forenoon watch to-morrow, and we shall both be off duty after general quarters. If you please, I will meet you at that time."

Somers considered a moment, and assented to the proposition. Pillgrim bade him good night, and retired to his own state-room, apparently without a fear that his victim would struggle in the trap into which he had fallen.

"And into the counsels of the ungodly enter thou not." This text rang in the mind of Somers, as though some mighty prophet were thundering it into his ears. He felt that he had already plunged deep enough into the pit of treason, and he was anxious to get away from it before he was scorched by the fire, and before the smell of fire clung to his garments.

For half an hour the fourth lieutenant of the Chatauqua sat at his desk, in deep thought. Though in the matter of which he was thinking, he had not sinned against his country, or the moral law, he was sorely troubled. He could not conceal from himself the fact that he was afraid of Pillgrim. The dread of having his name connected with any treasonable transaction was hard to overcome. That oath of allegiance, with his signature forged upon it, haunted him like an evil demon. He felt more timid and fearful than ever before in his life. His faith in Him who doeth all things well, seemed to be momentarily shaken, and he was hardly willing to do justly, and leave the consequences to themselves.

He felt weak, and being conscious of his weakness, he looked upward for strength. Leaning on his desk, he prayed for wisdom to know the right, and for the power to do it. He was in earnest; and though his prayer was not spoken, it moved his soul down to the depths of his spiritual being.

Three bells struck while he was thus engaged. He rose from the desk, and walked up and down the stateroom several times. Suddenly he stopped short. A great thought struck him. In an instant it became a great resolution. Before it had time to grow cold, he put on his coat and cap, and went out into the wardroom. Mr. Transit, the master, Mr. Grynbock, the paymaster, and Dr. De Plesion, the surgeon, were there, discussing the anticipated attacks on Mobile and Wilmington. Somers felt no interest in the conversation at this time. He went on deck, where he found Captain Cascabel and the first lieutenant, smoking their cigars. Waiting till the captain went below, he touched his cap to Mr. Hackleford.

"Mr. Somers?"

"Yes, sir."

"Not turned in, Mr. Somers? You have the mid-watch."

"If you will excuse me, sir, for coming to you at such a time, I wish to have half an hour's conversation with you."

"With me?" said Mr. Hackleford, apparently much surprised at such a request at such an hour.

"Yes, sir. It is a matter of the utmost consequence, or I would not have mentioned it at this time."

"Very well, Mr. Somers; I am ready to hear you."

"Excuse me, sir; I would rather not introduce the matter on deck."

"Well, come to my state-room."

"To my state-room, if you please, Mr. Hackleford."

"Why not mine?"

"I am afraid the person most deeply concerned will overhear me. His room is next to yours."

"Mr. Pillgrim?" exclaimed the first lieutenant.

"Yes, sir."

"Mr. Somers, I have a high regard for you as an officer and a gentleman, and I am not unacquainted with your past history. I hope you have nothing to say which will reflect on a brother officer."

"I have, sir."

"Then I advise you to think well before you speak."

"I am entirely prepared to speak, sir."

"Complaints against superior officers, Mr. Somers, are rather dangerous."

"It is not personal, sir, though I may be the sufferer for making it."

Mr. Hackleford led the way down to the ward-room. The officers had retired to their apartments, and there was no one to see them enter the state-room. As it was now nearly ten o'clock, when all officers' lights must be extinguished, Somers formally asked and obtained permission to burn his lamp till eleven o'clock. The first lieutenant entered the room, and Somers closed the door.

"Mr. Hackleford, may I trouble you to read this statement?" said Somers, as he handed out the paper he had so carefully prepared.

The first lieutenant adjusted his eye-glass, and read the statement through, asking an explanation of two or three points as he proceeded. He was deeply absorbed in the narrative, which was drawn up with the utmost minuteness.

"This is an infernal scheme, Mr. Somers. I hope you did not permit the vessel to sail without giving information of her character."

"The Ben Nevis sailed from New York before I could do anything or say a word," said Somers, exhibiting Langdon's letter.

"That was bad. You should have spoken before."

"My paper explains my reasons for keeping still. Perhaps I was wrong, sir, but I did the best I knew how."

"And this vessel is bound to Mobile. We may pick her up."

"The note says she is bound to Mobile; but it is not true. That is a blind to deceive me."

"Why should they wish to deceive you, after giving you their confidence."

"I don't know the reason."

"But what has all this to do with Mr. Pillgrim?" asked Mr. Hackleford.

"Mr. Pillgrim is the person spoken of in that paper as Coles."

"Impossible!" ejaculated Mr. Hackleford, springing to his feet.

"I shall be able to prove it by to-morrow, sir."

Somers then gave him the substance of the conversation between himself and Mr. Pillgrim.

"Why, this Coles wants something of you."

"Yes, sir; but I don't know what. He engaged to meet me here at four bells in the forenoon watch to-morrow, when he will tell me what he wants."

"Very well, Mr. Somers; meet him as agreed. You have played your part well. When you come together, you must yield the point; lead him along, and you will bag him,—and the vessel, I hope."

"The Ben Nevis will sail from St. John July 4, for Wilmington."

"Ah, then she is about even with the Chatauqua. I would give a year's pay for the privilege of catching her."

Until eleven o'clock the two officers consulted charts, and figured up the time of the Ben Nevis.

CHAPTER XI.

AFTER GENERAL QUARTERS.

AT eleven o'clock, when the master-at-arms knocked at the door of the fourth lieutenant, to inform him that it was time to put out his light, the calculations in regard to the position of the Ben Nevis had been made and verified. Mr. Hackleford, after counselling prudence and precaution, retired to his state-room. Somers threw himself on his cot, and having eased his mind of the heavy burden which had rested upon it, he went to sleep. But there was only an hour of rest for him, for at twelve o'clock he was to take the deck.

When eight bells struck, he turned out, much refreshed by his short nap, to relieve Mr. Garboard. It was a beautiful night, with only a gentle breeze from the westward, and the ship was doing her ten knots without making any fuss about it. Somers took the trumpet, which the officer of the deck always carries as the emblem of his office, and commenced his walk on the weather side.

Though he carefully watched the compasses, and saw that the sheets were hauled close home, he could not help thinking of the startling events which had transpired on the preceding evening. But he was satisfied with himself now. He had purged himself of all appearance of complicity with the enemies of his country, and he fully expected that Pillgrim would be put under arrest within the next forty-eight hours. The consciousness of duty done made him happy and contented. The first lieutenant had even praised him for the manner in which he had conducted the delicate business, and did not lay any stress on the oath of allegiance, or the commander's commission.

For his four hours he "planked the deck," thinking of the past and hopeful of the future. At eight bells he sent a midshipman down to call Mr. Pillgrim. While he was waiting to be relieved, he could not help considering what a risk it was to leave that noble ship in the hands of a traitor; but Somers had given all the information he had to Mr. Hackleford, and the responsibility did not rest upon himself. The first lieutenant was an able and discreet officer, and would not permit the Chatauqua to be imperilled even for a moment.

"Good morning, Mr. Somers," said Lieutenant Pillgrim, as he came on deck.

"Good morning, Mr. Pillgrim," replied Somers, with all the courtesy due to the quarter deck.

"A fine morning."

"Beautiful weather."

"You have had a good opportunity to think over our business. How do you feel about it?"

"Just right, I hope."

"I am glad to hear it. Have you seen anything of the Ben Nevis?"

"Of the Ben Nevis! No, sir; I don't expect to see her here."

"We may," replied Pillgrim, as he took the trumpet.

"Isn't she going to Mobile?"

"We'll talk of her during the forenoon watch," added the second lieutenant, as he turned on his heel and walked forward.

Somers went below. As he entered the ward-room, Mr. Hackleford came out of his state-room. This gentleman evidently intended to keep a sharp lookout for the officer of the deck during his watch. He asked the relieved officer if anything more had transpired; and the unimportant conversation which had just taken place was fully reported to him.

"Mr. Somers, I haven't slept an hour during the night. There are one or two points in your statement which were a little dark to me," said Mr. Hackleford.

"More than that of it is dark to me. I do not profess to understand the whole of it. I only state the facts from my own point of view."

" You listened to this talk between Coles and Langdon at the sailors' boarding-house in Front Street?"

" Yes, sir."

" If you saw Coles there, how could —"

" I didn't see him, sir ; I only heard him."

" That accounts for it," said Mr. Hackleford, musing. " Didn't you recognize Mr. Pillgrim's voice?"

" No, sir; I think he changed it; though the two tones were so similar that I might have recognized it, if I had suspected they were the same person."

Mr. Hackleford asked other questions, which Somers answered with strict regard to the truth, rather than with the intention of removing the first lieutenant's doubts. He wanted only facts himself, and he was careful not to distort them, in order to confirm any theory of his own or of his superior officer.

Mr. Hackleford went on deck, and Somers turned in. He was in condition to sleep now, and he improved his four hours below to the best advantage.

After general quarters, when the crew were dismissed, he went down to his state-room, prepared to meet Mr. Pillgrim. He was surprised to know how little curiosity he felt to learn what the traitor wanted and expected of him. Punctual to the appointed time, which exhibited the interest he felt in the expected interview, the treacherous second lieutenant made his appearance. Somers received him as one officer should receive another, though it was hard work for him to disguise the contempt and detestation with which he regarded the traitor.

"Well, Somers, now I am to tell you what I want of you. It isn't much, as I warned you before; and I am very glad to see that you are in such a happy frame of mind."

"I am ready to hear you, and do the best I can," replied Somers, carefully following the instructions of Mr. Hackleford with regard to matter and manner.

He had been cautioned to be ready enough in listening to the chief conspirator, but not too ready, so as to betray his object.

"Good! I think you understand me now."

"I think I do, sir."

"I am sorry to do it, but it is necessary for me to remind you again that your fate is in my hands; that a word from me would subject you to a trial by court martial for treason, and probably to more hemp rope than would feel good about your neck."

"Though I don't think I am in so much danger as you represent, I will grant your position."

"Don't grant it, if you think it is not correct;" and Mr. Pillgrim minutely detailed the evidence which could be brought to bear against him.

Somers appeared to be overwhelmed by this array of testimony. He groaned, looked hopeless, and finally granted the traitor's position in full.

"I am in your power. Do with me as you will. Of course the moment I put my foot on a rebel deck I am ruined."

"You can do as you please about going into the Confederate service. What I want of you will not compromise you as a loyal man in the slightest degree."

"What do you want of me?"

"Not quite so loud, if you please, Mr. Somers," said the lieutenant, glancing at the door. "To me, Somers, you have been a thorn. You lost me the Snowden, and the valuable cargo of the Theban."

"I only did my duty," pleaded Somers.

"Bah! don't use that word to me again. Through you a fortune slipped through my fingers. I should have got the Snowden into Wilmington, if you had not meddled with the matter. I have lost eighty thousand dollars by you."

"Of course I had no ill will against you personally."

"Very true; if you had, you would have been a dead man before this time. Phil Kennedy was a fool, but he was my best friend. I have his bond for forty thousand dollars, which is waste paper just now. Phil fell by your hand."

"It was in fair fight."

"Nonsense! What matter is it to me how he fell, whether it was in fair fight or foul? He is dead; that is all."

"What has all this to do with me?" asked Somers, with seeming impatience.

"Much, my dear fellow. Phil was to marry Kate Portington; was to pocket her fortune. You have cut him out. You will marry her, and in due time come into possession of a million. The commodore is apoplectic, and will not live many years. Do you see my point?"

"I do not," answered Somers, disgusted with this heartless statement.

"As you cheated me out of the Snowden, as you killed Phil Kennedy, as you will marry Kate Portington, I propose that you assume and pay Phil's bond."

"I?"

"Certainly — you; Mr. Somers; Kate's prodigy," laughed Pillgrim.

"Never!" exclaimed Somers, jumping to his feet.

"You speak too loud, Mr. Somers."

"Am I a dog, or a snake, or a toad, that I should do such an unclean thing?"

The traitor took from his pocket the oath of allegiance, opened it, and in silence thrust it into his companion's face.

"I have sold myself."

"You have, Somers. Think of it. If I have to make out a case against you, of course you will never see Kate again. Let me add, that the commodore sets his life by me. We were old friends before the war. You may marry his daughter with my consent, but not without it."

"I never thought of such a thing."

"Perhaps not. We waste time. Will you sign the bond?"

"The bond is good for nothing. No court —"

"That is my affair. If you agree to it, I will run all risks. I trouble no courts. If you don't pay, I have only to speak, and hang you then."

"I am lost," groaned Somers.

"No, you are not. Sign, and you have found fortune and a friend."

"I dare not sign."

"You dare not refuse."

Somers walked up and down the state-room, apparently in great mental agony.

"Shall I sign?" said he, in a loud tone, as though he were speaking to the empty air.

"Not so loud, man!" interposed Pillgrim, angrily.

At that instant two light raps were distinctly heard.

"What's that?" demanded the traitor, greatly alarmed.

"I will sign it," promptly added Somers, to whom the two raps seemed to be perfectly intelligible.

"What was that noise?" asked Pillgrim, fearfully. "Is there any one in Garboard's state-room?"

"I think not."

The second lieutenant was not satisfied. He opened

the door and looked into the adjoining state-room, but there was no person there, and the ward-room was empty. There was no one within hearing, and the conspirator recovered his wonted self-possession.

"You will sign?" said he.

"I will."

"I knew you would, and therefore I prepared the document; read it," he continued, taking a paper from his pocket.

Somers read. It was simply an agreement to pay forty thousand dollars, when he married Kate Portington, in consideration of certain assistance rendered the signer, but without any allusion to the circumstances under which it was given. As a legal document, of course it was good for nothing, as both parties well understood. Somers signed it.

"Now, Mr. Somers, we are friends," said Pillgrim, as he folded up the paper, and restored it to his pocket. "You have done me a good turn, and I have done you one."

Somers, unwilling to regard Pillgrim as a fool, believed that this paper was intended to ruin him in the estimation of the Portington family, and that the villain intended to marry her himself when her apparent suitor was disposed of.

"Is this all you expect of me?" asked Somers.

"This is the principal thing. I may have occasion to

use you again; if I do, I shall not hesitate to call upon you. You are in my confidence now."

"Will you tell me, then, where the Ben Nevis is bound? I may want to find her, for I haven't much taste for the old navy now."

"Ah, you make better progress than I anticipated. She is bound to St. Marks."

This was a lie, as Somers well knew.

"Coles and Langdon said she was to make Mobile."

"The plan was changed. You must not lay much stress on what you heard that night. It was all a blind, — or most of it was."

"Indeed?"

"The conversation at the house in Front Street was carried on for your especial benefit," added Pillgrim, laughing and rubbing his hands. "Langdon wrote both letters about the wounded sailor; there was no such person. The old woman that kept the house was in my pay. When I spoke so warmly in your praise to Langdon, I knew that you were listening to all I said; indeed, I said it to you rather than to Langdon."

"Why did you tell me beforehand, if you intended to catch me with the treasonable offer?" asked Somers, rather mortified to learn that he had been duped from the beginning.

"I knew you would pretend to accept it. All I wanted was to get you to take the commission, orders, and oath. As you agreed to sign the latter, Langdon did it for you, for I could not wait."

"The Ben Nevis is no humbug?"

"No; I bought her and two other steamers on the Clyde, in Scotland. The Ben Nevis was captured, but my friends bought her after she was condemned. As there had been a great deal said about her in the newspapers, I used her because it was probable you had heard of her."

"I had."

"Everything works as I intended."

"Not exactly," thought Somers.

"The captain of the coaster that pounded you that night was Langdon," laughed Pilgrim.

"Why was that done?"

"That I might take you back to the hotel, and be your friend. We did not intend to hurt you much. It was important that you should think well of me. You do — don't you?"

"Of course."

"All right now; remember you are mine, Somers," said Pillgrim, as he left the room.

CHAPTER XII.

THE BEN NEVIS.

THE Chatauqua rolled along easily on her course during the rest of the day, until the dog watch, when Mr. Pillgrim had the deck again. Somers, having discharged his whole duty in reference to the conspiracy, was content to leave the matter in the hands of Mr. Hackleford, to whom he had committed it.

At eight bells, as soon as Somers had been relieved from the afternoon watch, he was not a little surprised to receive a message from the captain, inviting him to his cabin. He readily came to the conclusion that the summons related to the conspiracy. When he entered the cabin, he saw Captain Cascabel and Mr. Hackleford seated at the table, on which was spread a general chart of the coast of the United States.

"Say what you wish to Mr. Somers," said the captain to the first lieutenant.

"Mr. Somers, Captain Cascabel has sent for you in relation to the affair of which we talked in your stateroom last night." Mr Hackleford began "All that you have written out in your statement, and all that you told me, have been fully confirmed."

"I intended to confine myself strictly to the facts," replied Somers, modestly.

"You have been very discreet and very prudent," added Mr. Hackleford.

"I fully concur," said Captain Cascabel. "You have exposed yourself to no little peril, in your zeal to serve your country."

Somers bowed and blushed.

"I confess that I had some doubts in regard to the result of your operations, Mr. Somers," continued the first lieutenant; "but I am entirely satisfied now that Mr. Pillgrim is just what you represent him to be."

"All that you affirmed has been fully verified," added the captain.

He did not say that both himself and Mr. Hackleford had listened to the entire conversation between Somers and the traitor in the forenoon, occupying one of the captain's state-rooms, which adjoined the starboard side of the ward-room, having bored a couple of holes through the partition, behind the bureau; he did not say this, for it was hardly dignified for a captain to play the cavesdropper, even in a good cause. Somers knew that Mr. Hackleford was at hand at the time, and had arranged a set of signals by which he could advise the young officer, if he should be in doubt. One rap meant, " No ; " two raps, " Yes ; " and three raps, " Give no direct answer." When Somers was in doubt respecting the bond, he asked the question of the empty air, apparently, but really of Mr. Hackleford, who had promptly replied in the affirmative by giving the two knocks, which had startled the traitor.

"Mr. Somers, what do you know of the Ben Nevis?" asked the captain.

"She was to sail from St. John on the 4th of July, to run the blockade at Wilmington. She is said to make sixteen knots, under favorable circumstances."

"She has had a head wind part of the time. If she has made twelve on the average, she has done well," said Mr. Hackleford.

"She will be due off Cape Fear some time after meridian to-morrow," added the captain, consulting a paper, on which were several arithmetical operations.

The calculations were carefully reviewed, and Somers was questioned at considerable length; but he had already given all the information he possessed. It was evidently the intention of Captain Cascabel to capture the Ben Nevis, though he did not announce his purpose.

"After what has occurred, Mr. Somers, you may be surprised that Mr. Pillgrim has not been relieved from duty and placed under arrest," continued Captain Cascabel, after the position of the Ben Nevis had been carefully estimated.

"I leave the matter entirely in the hands of my superior officers," replied Somers. "Having cast the responsibility upon them, I am willing to obey orders without asking any questions."

"That is a very proper view to take of the subject, and I commend your moderation," said the captain, with a pleasant smile. "It has been thought best not to disturb Mr. Pillgrim for a day or two, for other events may transpire."

Captain Cascabel bowed to Somers, and intimated that he had no further need of him at present.

"Ah, Mr. Somers, been visiting the captain," said the second lieutenant, as his victim came on deck.

"I was sent for."

"What was the business?"

Fortunately, Mr. Transit, who was planking the deck on the lee side, approached near enough to enable Somers to avoid answering the question, and he thus escaped the necessity of telling a falsehood. But as soon as Mr. Garboard took the deck, Pillgrim repeated the inquiry, and the young officer was obliged to narrate an imaginary conversation.

"It's no matter, Somers. You understand that I have a rope round your neck, and I am not at all afraid that you will make an improper use of your tongue."

"I certainly shall not," answered Somers, with emphasis. "You may depend upon me for that."

"The fact is, Somers, I have got a mortgage on you, and I want no better security for your good conduct."

"You needn't trouble yourself at all about me."

"I shall not; because, if you wish to betray me, I should rather enjoy it. I have been your best friend. Instead of blowing your brains out for making an end of poor Phil Kennedy, I have taken you into my confidence. You shall marry the prettiest and the richest girl north of the Potomac; and when Union officers are proscribed and condemned after the war, you will have a friend at court who will speak a good word for you."

"Thank you; but do you really believe that the South will carry the day?"

"I'm sure of it. England is our best friend; and Louis Napoleon, in order to complete his Mexican scheme, must recognize the Confederacy. When France does the job, England will be only one day behind her."

"If I go with you, I shall be on the winning side, then."

"If you do? You have gone with me. Though I don't ask you to help the South openly, I expect you to be a friend of the government which must soon rule the country. Leave it all to me, Somers, and I will manage the business for you and myself. You must confess, Somers, that I am a little ahead of you in strategy," said the traitor, with a complacent smile.

"You beat me in the game we have been playing; but

that only makes us even, for I got the better of you in another affair."

"Not of me; it was the stupidity of Phil Kennedy that ruined the Snowden business. I pride myself on my strategy, Somers. I have never been beaten in anything of this kind yet. The fact of it is, I know whom to trust. I never give my confidence to a man who dares to betray it," replied Pillgrim, rubbing his hands with delight at his own cleverness.

Somers was of the opinion that he would think differently before many days had elapsed; but he was as prudent as the circumstances required.

At eight bells, the fourth lieutenant took the deck for the first watch; and from that time until the following afternoon, he saw but little of the conspirator. At this time, the ship was off Cape Fear, though too far out to sight the land, or even the outer line of blockaders which kept vigilant watch over the entrance to the river. Precisely at the moment when one bell struck in the first dog-watch, the engine of the Chatauqua, without any order from the officer of the deck, and without any apparent reason, suddenly stopped.

It had proved itself to be a very good and well-meaning engine, thus far, and all hands began to wonder what had happened, or what was going to happen. But Mr. Cranklin, the chief engineer, presently reported that there was a "screw loose" somewhere, and that it would be necessary to lay to, and make some repairs. Certainly it was a very opportune moment for the ship to stop; and those who did not know what had passed between the chief engineer and the first lieutenant might have supposed that the zealous engine, heretofore so faithful in the discharge of its trying duties, had overheard some of the conversation we have related, and was waiting for the Ben Nevis to show herself to seaward.

In further confirmation that the stoppage was not entirely owing to the obstinacy of the engine, it was observed that extra lookout men had been stationed on the fore yard, and on the cross-trees, since meridian of that day. The captain and the first lieutenant were often seen in confidential communication; and everybody on board seemed to be impressed with the idea that something was about to "turn up."

Something did "turn up," about three bells; for the man on the fore cross-trees, reported a vessel on the beam. The dense mass of black smoke in the wake of her smoke-stack indicated that she was an English blockade runner, approaching the coast so as to run in after dark. As soon as this agreeable information spread through the Chatauqua, it created an intense excitement, not manifested in noisy demonstrations, for that would have been in violation of the strict rule of naval discipline, but in the expectant eyes and stimulated movements of the officers and crew, to whose pockets, as well as to their national pride, the prospect of a rich prize appealed with tremendous force.

At this thrilling moment, when everything depended upon the sailing qualities of the Chatauqua, either Mr. Cranklin had completed his remedial efforts, or the engine had come to a realizing sense of the proprieties of the occasion, and was sensible of the appalling wickedness of disappointing the two hundred and fifty anxious souls on board. The docile machine was reported to be in condition for active service. The bells pealed forth the signal to "go ahead slowly," then "at full speed," and the Chatauqua darted away.

"Hard a starboard!" said Mr. Somers, now the officer of the deck, to the quartermaster, who was conning the wheel.

"Hard a starboard, sir!"

"Steady!"

"Steady, sir!"

"What does this mean, Somers?" demanded Pillgrim, in a low, angry tone, as he passed the officer of the deck.

"I don't know, sir. I only obey orders," replied Somers, as he glanced ahead at the chase.

"Do you know what steamer that is?" asked Pillgrim.

"How should I?"

"It is the Ben Nevis."

"How do you know?"

"I know; that is sufficient. We must save her," said the second lieutenant, in low, but excited tones.

The chase continued for half an hour longer, when it was evident that the Ben Nevis — for it was indeed she — had changed her course, and was headed to the eastward.

"This will never do, Mr. Somers," said Mr. Hackleford. "We can't sail with her. We must change our tactics."

"She gains upon us," replied Somers.

"No doubt of it."

"I am afraid we shall lose her, sir."

"I would give my year's pay to capture her, Mr. Somers, if it were only for your sake."

Somers suggested an idea to the first lieutenant, who, after the approval of Captain Cascabel, adopted it.

"Clear away the first cutter," said Mr. Hackleford. "Lower away."

The first cutter was soon in the water, the ship having now stopped her engine.

"Mr. Pillgrim, you will stand by in the first cutter till that steamer comes up. Capture her if her papers are not all right, or if she is bound into Wilmington."

A smile of satisfaction lighted up the countenance of the second lieutenant, when he found he was to go in the boat. The first cutter pulled away.

"Clear away the second cutter!" said the first lieutenant: and while the men were eagerly performing this duty, the captain instructed Somers, who was to go in her, in regard to the duty he was expected to perform.

Somers took his place in the stern-sheets of the second cutter, which was armed with a twenty-four pounder howitzer, while the first cutter had nothing but small arms. As soon as this boat left the ship's side, the Chatauqua came about, as though she had abandoned the chase, and stood to the westward.

The Ben Nevis immediately discovered the change which had been made in the course of her pursuer. Apparently satisfied that she had outwitted the man-of-war, she put about and headed towards the coast again, without suspecting the fact that two boats lay in her track.

CHAPTER XIII.

A CONFLICT OF AUTHORITY.

IT was about sunset when the Ben Nevis put about and headed in shore. The first cutter was at least half a mile in advance of the second, and both of them lying near the track of the blockade-runner. It was useless to pull towards the expected prize; on the contrary, it was better policy to keep still, so as not to attract the attention of her people.

The Ben Nevis, when she changed her course, might have been about five miles distant from the Chatauqua, and the longer the meeting between the steamer and the boats was deferred, the more would the darkness favor the latter. It was thought that the blockade-runner would approach at half speed, so as not to encounter the fleet off the river at too early an hour; but her commander did not appear to regard this delay as necessary, and came down at full speed. It was not dark, therefore, when the first cutter was within hail of her.

As soon as the Ben Nevis discovered the nearest boat,

she sheered off, though, as the first cutter had no howitzer, she could have everything her own way. Somers kept the second cutter just out of hail of the other boat; and carefully watched the operations of the second lieutenant.

The steamer sheered off just enough to avoid the boat; but presently she resumed her course, as if, making twelve knots, she had nothing to fear from an enemy with oars only to urge her forward. It would be impossible for the first cutter to board her at full speed, and she seemed disposed to run the risk of a shot or two rather than expose herself to falling into any other trap which the man-of-war might have set for her.

The Ben Nevis dashed on, therefore, in a direction which placed the first cutter on her starboard bow, when Mr. Pillgrim hailed her, and ordered her to heave to, accompanying the command with a peculiar wave of his cap in the air, which was thrice repeated, very much to the astonishment, no doubt, of the loyal blue-jackets in the boat with him.

"Topple my timber-heads! What does all that mean?" exclaimed Boatswain Longstone, who, by the especial request of the fourth lieutenant, had a place in the stern-sheets of the second cutter.

"Wait, and you will see," replied Mr. Somers.

The Ben Nevis at once stopped her wheels, and the first cutter pulled towards her.

"That beats me!" ejaculated the boatswain. "What did she stop for?"

"Probably her captain thinks that is his best course," replied Somers, who knew very well why she had stopped.

The commander of the blockade-runner evidently recognized the voice and the signal of Pillgrim, and, like an obedient servant, was willing to shift the responsibility of the occasion on his owner and employer. Honest Tom Longstone was sorely perplexed by the movement of the steamer and the conduct of the second lieutenant of the Chatauqua, for a suspicion of foul play on the part of one of his officers could not have entered his loyal heart.

The first cutter touched the side of the Ben Nevis, and Mr. Pillgrim went up the accommodation ladder.

"Clear away the howitzer!" said Somers.

The boatswain looked at him as though he had been mad.

"Man the howitzer!"

The gun was loaded with a solid shot, and made ready for instant use.

"Now give way, boatswain," continued Somers; and the second cutter dashed swiftly over the long billows towards the Ben Nevis.

"Are you going to use that gun?" asked Tom Longstone, in a low tone.

"If necessary."

"But Mr. Pillgrim has the steamer. He has boarded her."

"We will wait and see," answered Somers, evasively; for it was expected and intended that the second lieutenant should "hang himself," on this interesting occasion.

Before the second cutter could reach the steamer, Mr. Pillgrim had completed his examination on board of her, and descended to his boat. As he gave the order for the cutter to shove off, Somers's boat shot in alongside of her.

"She is all right, Mr. Somers," said the second lieutenant.

"All right?" exclaimed Somers; and, in spite of himself, he actually trembled with emotion, being conscious that a very trying scene was before him — one which would require all his skill and all his energy.

"I say she is all right, Mr. Somers," repeated Pillgrim, sharply, for he did not appear to like the tone and manner of the fourth lieutenant.

"What is she?"

"She is an American steamer from Baltimore, bound to Havana."

"What is she doing in here, then?" demanded Somers.

"That's her affair. Don't you see the American flag at her peak?"

"What is her name?"

"The Ben Nevis," replied Pillgrim, with the most expressive emphasis. "Sheer off, and return to the ship."

"I think she is a blockade-runner."

"Do you, indeed?" sneered the traitor.

"I am satisfied she is."

"I have boarded her, and my report will be final in this matter."

"My orders were to board her," said Somers.

"Your orders?"

"Yes, sir."

"I am your superior officer.

"You are, Mr. Pillgrim."

"Of course your orders were intended to be carried out, in case you happened to come up with the steamer before I did."

"I was ordered to board her, Mr. Pillgrim, and I feel compelled to obey," replied Somers, with firmness, though he still trembled with emotion.

"Steady, Mr. Somers; be careful," said Tom Longstone, bewildered by this conflict of authority — a circumstance he had not before observed in his long career in the navy. "He is your superior officer."

"I know what I am about, Tom," whispered Somers, compassionating the misery his apparently mutinous actions must cause his honest friend.

"If you do, go ahead, my darling."

"Mr. Somers, I order you to return to the ship," said Mr. Pillgrim, sternly.

"I must obey the captain's orders, and board this steamer."

"You mistake your orders, and I insist that you obey me."

"You will excuse me if I disregard your command; and I will be answerable to the captain for my conduct."

"The captain is not here; I am your superior officer. Disobey me at your peril!" continued Pillgrim, in savage tones.

"Is it all right?" shouted the captain of the Ben Nevis, who was standing on the starboard paddle-box of the steamer.

"Ay, ay; all right. Start your wheels!" replied Pillgrim.

"Captain, if you move a wheel, I will fire into you!" added Somers; and the captain of the howitzer stood, with the lock-string in his hand, ready to execute the order when it should be given.

The commander of the Ben Nevis looked down upon the second cutter's gun, pointing into the hull of his vessel, so that the twenty-four pound shot would pass through her engine-room. He did not give the order to start the wheels. Pillgrim was disconcerted: he was foiled in his scheme. By this time he realized that the fourth lieutenant of the Chatauqua was not the willing, timid tool he had taken him to be.

The men in both boats were astonished and confounded by the startling clash of authority between their officers. Such a thing had never been known before. They had been surprised when Mr. Pillgrim declared that the steamer was all right, for there was not one of them who was not perfectly satisfied that the vessel was running in to break the blockade. They were still more surprised when Mr. Somers dared to dispute the conclusious of his superior officer. Involuntarily they took sides with the fourth lieutenant, because his opinion that the Ben Nevis was not all right coincided with their own, and because the prize-money went with his view of the matter. But they were well disciplined men, and each crew, thus far, obeyed the orders of its own officer; and, so far as they were concerned, there was no conflict of command, though this was likely soon to be the case.

"Mr. Somers, I warn you — beware!" said Pillgrim, with the most expressive emphasis.

"I intend to do my duty," replied Somers.

"Bully for the fourth luff!" shouted a seaman in the second cutter, who felt disposed to take a part in the dispute.

"Silence!" interposed Somers, sternly, as he perceived that this bad example was likely to be followed by others.

and he felt that the occasion was too serious and solemn to admit of anything like levity.

"Mr. Somers, you know the consequences!" continued the second lieutenant.

"I do."

"Remember!"

"I know what I am about," answered Somers, understanding to what Pillgrim alluded, though of course it was incomprehensible to others in the boats. "I shall board the steamer."

"Do it at your peril!"

"I shall do it."

"This is mutiny!" stormed Pillgrim, with an oath, as he took a revolver from his belt.

"I will abide the consequences," replied Somers, drawing his pistol.

"For God's sake, Mr. Somers —"

"Silence, boatswain!"

"You will ruin yourself," whispered Tom, whose bronzed face was ghastly pale, and whose lips quivered with the anxiety he felt for his *protégé*.

"I am perfectly cool, Tom; don't be alarmed about me," replied Somers, tenderly, as he glanced at the expression of suffering on the face of his faithful friend. "That man is a traitor!" he whispered.

"Once more, Mr. Somers, will you obey me, or will you not?" shouted Mr. Pillgrim, angrily.

"If you will capture this steamer, as you should do, I will obey you in all things," replied Somers. "I know she is about to run the blockade, and so do you."

"I have examined her, and I declare that her papers are all right. My decision is final. Return to the ship, Mr. Somers, and there answer for your mutinous conduct."

"I shall board this vessel," replied Somers, as he ordered the bowman to haul in towards the steamer.

"This is mutiny, and I shall treat it as such. I *will* be obeyed!"

Mr. Pillgrim raised his pistol, and fired at the rebellious officer; but he was too much excited to take good aim, if, indeed, he intended to do anything more than intimidate his inferior officer. The ball whistled within a few feet of Somers's head, and roused his belligerent spirit. He raised his revolver on the instant, before the second lieutenant was ready to repeat his experiment, and fired.

The traitor sank down in the stern-sheets of the cutter. The men seemed to be paralyzed by this sharp work, and sat like statues on the thwarts.

"Haul in, bowman!" said Somers, in sharp and earnest tones, breaking the solemn silence of that awful moment.

The man obeyed mechanically, and the others did the same when required to boat their oars; but probably there was not one of the crew of either cutter who did not believe that the fourth lieutenant would be hung at the yard-arm for his mutinous, murderous conduct.

Somers directed the coxswain of the first cutter to pull in to the accommodation ladder of the steamer. He was obeyed, and Boatswain Longstone was ordered to take charge of the boat. Eight men, armed with cutlasses and revolvers, were sent on board the Ben Nevis, and Somers followed them. The captain protested against the capture, but his papers were not what they were represented to be by Pillgrim. The character of the steamer was evident, and she was taken possession of by the fourth lieutenant, and the crews of both cutters were ordered on board.

"How is Mr. Pillgrim?" asked Somers of the boatswain. "Is he dead?"

"No, sir; the ball only glanced along the side of his head. He bleeds badly, but he is not severely wounded."

The second lieutenant was soon able to sit up, and was assisted on board the Ben Nevis, where he was conducted to a state-room, and two seamen placed as guards at the door.

"Somers, you have played me false!" said Pillgrim, with a savage expression on his pale face, "but you are a doomed man."

"As you please, Mr. Pillgrim. You will consider yourself under arrest," replied Somers, as the traitor passed into his state-room.

CHAPTER XIV.

THE PRIZE STEAMER.

IT was quite dark when the capture of the Ben Nevis was completed. Rockets were thrown up to inform the Chatauqua of her present position, and with guards of seamen in the engine and firerooms, the wheels of the captured steamer were set in motion, and she was headed to the north. Somers displayed his usual decision and energy, and perhaps the men began to think, by this time, that the young officer knew his duty and was competent to perform it.

While the Ben Nevis was making her way towards the Chatauqua, Somers paced the deck, thinking of the great event which had just transpired. The captain of the Ben Nevis, sullen and discontented, stood by the quartermaster at the wheel. He had attempted to enter the state-room of the wounded officer, but the seamen in charge of the prisoner had been instructed to exclude him, and they carefully obeyed their orders.

The men of the first and second cutters were silent and troubled. Perhaps they fully sympathized with Somers, and dreaded the consequence of the decisive deed he had performed. However the petty officers and seamen felt, it is quite certain that Boatswain Longstone could hardly keep from weeping when he thought of the punishment which might be in store for his young friend. He was in charge of the lookouts forward, and when the Chatauqua was sighted, he went aft to report to Somers.

"Very well; we shall soon see the end of this business," said the young officer.

"I would like to see you safe through it," added the boatswain, in tones of unaffected sympathy.

"What's the matter, Tom?" asked Somers.

"I feel worse to-night than I have before for twenty odd years," groaned Tom.

"Why so?"

"I'm afraid this is bad business. It's no little thing to fire a pistol at your superior officer."

"I told you what he was."

"I know you said he was a traitor; but it don't do for an officer in the navy to take the law into his own hands."

"This steamer makes sixteen knots an hour, they say," said Somers, with a smile.

The boatswain looked at him, and wondered what this had to do with shooting the second lieutenant.

"She was going to run the blockade," continued Somers.

"No doubt of that."

"Then they intended to fit her out as a Confederate cruiser."

"Perhaps they did, Mr. Somers; you know best."

"Mr. Pillgrim did not intend to capture her."

"He did not, sartinly."

"Suppose I had permitted this vessel to go on her way, to run the blockade, which she could have done as easily as a hundred others have done the same thing, at the same place, and then come out as a man-of-war."

"But Mr. Pillgrim was your superior officer, and he was responsible, not you."

"I carried out my orders to the letter, Tom."

"Did you?"

"To the letter, I said."

"Were you ordered to shoot Mr. Pillgrim?"

"Yes, if necessary."

"Thank'ee, Mr. Somers. You have taken a weight heavier than the best bower off my stomach. I'd rather be where Jonah was — in the whale's belly — than see any harm come to you. I feel better now."

"You shall know all about it, Tom, in a few days, or perhaps a few hours."

"I'm satisfied, Mr. Somers. Shiver my kevel-heads, but I ought to have been satisfied with anything you do."

By this time the steamer came up with the Chatauqua, and both vessels stopped their engines, as the Ben Nevis rounded to under the stern of the man-of-war.

"Chatauqua, ahoy!" shouted Somers.

"On board the prize!" replied the officer of the deck.

"Send the surgeon on board, if you please."

"Ay, ay."

In a few moments the third cutter, in charge of Mr. Transit, the master, put off from the ship, with Dr. De Plesion on board.

"Where is Mr. Pillgrim, sir?" asked the master of Somers.

"Wounded, below."

"Mr. Hackleford wishes your report forthwith on board the ship."

"Mr. Transit, Mr. Pillgrim is under arrest. You will permit no one to communicate with him except the surgeon."

"Under arrest!" exclaimed Mr. Transit.

"I have no time to explain," replied Somers, as he directed his coxswain to pipe down his boat's crew.

When the second cutter was hauled up to the accommodation ladder, Somers stepped on board, and a few moments later, touched his hat to the first lieutenant on the quarter deck of the Chatauqua.

"I have to report that I have captured the Ben Nevis," said Somers.

"Where is Mr. Pillgrim?" asked Mr. Hackleford, the captain standing by, an interested and excited listener.

"He is wounded, and under arrest, sir."

"How wounded?"

"He fired at me, and in self-defence I was obliged to shoot him. I think he is not seriously wounded. He boarded the Ben Nevis, and had given the captain of her permission to proceed, though the vessel was headed towards Cape Fear."

"You have done well, Mr. Somers," said Captain Cascabel. "Beat to quarters, Mr. Hackleford."

When the crew were at quarters, Mr. Hackleford explained to them what had occurred, and fully justified the course of the fourth lieutenant; whereupon an earnest and enthusiastic cheer rang through the ship.

"Are you satisfied, Tom?" asked Somers of the boatswain.

"Bless ye! I was satisfied before, Mr. Somers. There is only one dark thing in the whole of it."

"What's that, Tom?"

"If Captain Cascabel and Mr. Hackleford both knew that Mr. Pillgrim was a traitor, why did they send him out to capture that steamer? That's what I can't see through."

"Can't you? Well, if they had not sent him, we should not have captured the Ben Nevis."

"I don't see why."

"Don't you? Well, you are not as sharp as you are sometimes."

"I know I'm dull, Mr. Somers, but splinter my figger head if I can see through it."

"The Ben Nevis is good for fifteen knots at least."

"I know that; she did it while we were coming up."

"The Chatauqua can't make more than twelve."

"That's true."

"Then, of course, the Chatauqua could not catch the Ben Nevis."

"That's clear enough. But we were out in the boats, and were close aboard of her."

"And just then she sheered off. Could the boats have overhauled her?"

"Sartinly not; but you could have put a shot through her hull."

"Which might, at that distance, have disabled her, and might not. The chances were all against us. But the moment Mr. Pillgrim hailed her, and swung his cap, she stopped her wheels. They knew very well he would not detain her."

"I see now."

"Probably the captain of the Ben Nevis knew the Chatauqua, and knew that Pillgrim was on board of her, and they were on the lookout for him. If any other officer than myself had been in the second cutter, I am satisfied Mr. Pillgrim would not have returned to his boat, but would have staid on board the Ben Nevis."

"He's a horrible villain — arn't he?" said the honest boatswain.

This conversation took place while Captain Cascabel

was preparing his despatches to be sent by the prize steamer to the navy department. When they were completed, Somers was sent for, and he repaired at once to the captain's cabin.

"Mr. Somers, though I can hardly spare you, I feel compelled to send you home as prize master in the Ben Nevis. I have commended you to the department," said Captain Cascabel, as he handed him the despatches.

"Thank you, sir."

A prize crew was at once detailed, with two master's mates to act as first and second officers, and a corporal and three marines to guard the prisoner who was to be sent back in the prize. Somers bade a hasty good by to his brother officers, and with his crew was sent on board the Ben Nevis, whose deck he was now to tread for a brief period as her commander. His orders required him to take the Ben Nevis to Fortress Monroe, and there communicate with the navy department.

"Well, doctor, how is your patient?" asked Somers, when he reached the deck of the prize.

"He will do very well. If you had put the bullet half an inch nearer his brain, you would have finished him. The skin is torn off the side of his head, and I suppose the ball stunned him. He is sitting up now, and appears to be as well as ever, though in no very amiable frame of mind."

"I suppose not."

"He says you are a rebel and a traitor, and he intends to prove it. I told him I thought his wound had affected his brain."

"It would require a long story to explain what he means. Mr. Hackleford has the papers, and I doubt not he will tell you all about it, doctor," replied Somers, as he proceeded to arrange for the return voyage.

All who were not going home in the Ben Nevis were sent back to the Chatauqua. The firemen and engineers of the prize steamer were willing to discharge their duties as before, and under the direction of one of the second assistants from the ship, they were set at work. The first and third cutters pulled away towards the man-of-war, giving three rousing cheers as they departed, and the Ben Nevis steamed away to the northward.

By this time it was ten o'clock at night. The watch was set on deck, and Somers went below to obtain his supper, for he felt the need of some rest and refreshment. The steward, anxious to be on good terms with the new commander, had provided the best meal the larder of the Ben Nevis afforded, and Somers was hungry enough to do it ample justice.

A marine, with cutlass and revolver, stood at the door of Pillgrim's state-room. When Somers had finished his supper, and was about to go on deck, the sentinel informed him that the prisoner had knocked several times on his door.

"See what he wants."

The marine opened the door.

"Who is the prize master?" asked Pillgrim.

The sentinel looked at Somers for permission before he replied.

"Answer him."

"Mr. Somers," answered the marine.

"Will you present my compliments to Mr. Somers, and say that I beg the favor of an interview with him?"

Again the sentinel glanced at Somers.

"With pleasure," replied the prize master, as politely as the request was made.

"Ah, Mr. Somers," said the traitor, as the new commander of the Ben Nevis stepped forward and showed himself to the prisoner, "I am happy to see you."

"Are you, indeed?" added Somers, rather amused at the smooth tones of the traitor.

"I am, I assure you. Might I beg the favor of a few moments' private conversation with you?"

"Certainly; have you any weapons about you?"

"None, whatever."

Somers directed the marine to seat himself at the farther end of the cabin.

"Thank you, Mr. Somers; you are as kind and generous as ever."

"Let me say, Mr. Pillgrim, that flattery and threats are all the same to me."

"Somers, you have me on the hip."

"I know it."

"You have won the game."

"I know it."

"I am in your power."

"I know it."

Pillgrim appeared to be hopeless and disconcerted.

"Somers, I have, in a bank in Philadelphia, fifty thousand dollars."

"What bank?"

"Excuse me; the confiscation laws are dangerous to men in my situation."

"No matter; I will inform the proper officers of the fact, and they can find out what bank."

Pillgrim bit his lip.

"I will give you this money if you will —"

"Silence, sir! There is not money enough in the whole world to bribe me."

"I still have the oath of allegiance — signed by you, and —"

"No, you haven't. Mr. Hackleford has it. You left it in your state-room."

"Now listen to reason, Somers."

"I shall. Reason counsels me to do my duty."

"Somers, I will be revenged."

"Good night, Mr. Pillgrim. I see you have nothing of importance to say to me;" and Somers went on deck after calling the marine back to his post.

CHAPTER XV.

THE PRISONER IN THE CABIN.

MR. PILLGRIM'S wound, as such injuries are regarded in the army and navy, was a mere scratch; but it might have been very sore, and might have ached severely. The traitor did not even mention it in his interview with Somers, for the sore in his mind was much more serious. His victim had now become his tyrant; not implacable or vindictive, but firm and unyielding in the discharge of his duty.

Somers went on deck, satisfied himself in regard to the course of the steamer, then visited the engine-room, and other parts of the vessel, until he had assured himself that everything was right. It was a fine, clear night, and when the port watch came on deck, he went below, and lay down on the broad sofa, which extended across the after part of the cabin. He was tired enough to sleep, and he did sleep till the starboard watch was called in the morning.

He was a prudent and zealous commander, and he

hastened on deck at once to make sure that his charge was still safe. The weather continued fine, and every man was at his post. He scrutinized the log slate, and questioned the officer of the deck. Everything had been correctly done; nothing had happened, and nothing was likely to happen. There was nothing for him to do but sleep, and he returned to his couch in the cabin, to complete his nap.

The sentinel at the door of the prisoner's state-room was still in position. The guard was relieved every two hours, and the door was secured on the outside by a padlock, which had been put on by the armorer after the vessel was captured. Of course there could be no doubt in regard to the safety of the prisoner.

Somers went to sleep again, satisfied that he had neglected no precautions to insure the safety of the vessel and the prisoner. The movements of the steward in the cabin awoke him at six o'clock. He had slept away all his fatigue, and when he looked out through the stern lights upon a smooth sea, brightened by the morning sun, all his anxiety left him. It was hardly possible that any accident could interfere with the safe arrival of the prize at her destined port.

As he rose from the sofa, the corporal of marines relieved the sentry at the prisoner's door.

"Marine," said Somers, as the man passed him on his way out of the cabin.

14 *

The sentinel stopped and touched his cap.

"How is the prisoner?"

"I haven't heard anything of him, sir, during my beat," replied the marine.

"Isn't he up yet?"

"I didn't hear him, sir. He's a heavy sleeper, I should say, for I don't think he moved while I was on guard."

As Somers had the key of the padlock in his pocket, he was satisfied it was all right with the prisoner, and he went on deck. At seven bells, when his breakfast was brought down, he directed the steward to give Mr. Pillgrim his morning meal, handing the key of the state-room to the corporal.

The door was opened, and the marine entered the little room. Somers sat down at the table to eat his breakfast. He was blessed with a good appetite, and some "'am and heggs," which the steward particularly recommended, looked very inviting. But he had hardly satisfied himself that the steward had not overrated the quality of his viands, before his attention was attracted by an exclamation from the corporal of marines.

"What's the matter?" demanded Somers, rising from the table, and rushing to the state-room.

"Mr. Pillgrim is not here, sir," replied the man.

"Not here!"

"No, sir."

"He can't be far off."

Somers entered the state-room. Certainly the prisoner was not there; nor was there any indication of the means by which he had departed. The partitions between this and the adjoining state-rooms were undisturbed. The door had been securely locked, and the key was in the pocket of the commanding officer. The traitor could not have crawled through the bull's eye which lighted the room, for it was not more than nine inches in diameter.

The marines who had been on guard during the night were summoned. They all told the same story; not a sound had been heard in the room. Both the master's mates who had kept the watches on deck were examined, but they had no information to communicate.

"This is very remarkable," said Somers to his first officer.

"Very remarkable," replied Mr. Hudson, who seemed to be even more bewildered than his commander.

"Where is Captain Walmsley?" asked Somers of the steward.

"I don't know, sir. I 'aven't seen him since 'e hat his supper last night."

"See if he is in his state-room, steward."

He was not in his state-room. His bed had not been occupied; no one had seen him since the Ben Nevis parted company with the Chatauqua.

"Are there any boats missing, Mr. Hudson?" continued Somers.

"No, sir; the steamer had two quarter-boats, and a life-boat forward. They are all in their places."

"Wasn't there a dingy, or a jolly-boat, at the stern?"

"No, sir; I am sure that no boat is missing."

"Then of course the prisoner must be on board."

"No doubt of that, Mr. Somers. In my opinion he has concealed himself in the hold, and intends to escape after we go into port."

"But how could he get into the hold?"

"That is more than I know, sir. He isn't in his state-room; he wouldn't have jumped overboard forty miles from land."

"He must be found before we make the capes," said Somers, who could not help thinking how "cheap" he should feel if compelled to report the escape of his prisoner to the department.

He returned to the table and finished his breakfast, as a matter of necessity now, — for man must eat, — rather than of inclination. The Scotch ham seemed to have lost its fine flavor, and it was really a pity that he had not completed his repast before the escape of Pillgrim was discovered. But Somers was satisfied that the traitor was still on board, and he was determined to find him, even if he had to throw the valuable cargo of the Ben Nevis overboard, in order to effect his purpose.

When Somers had worried down his breakfast, he went on deck to detail parties to engage in the search.

The hatches were taken off, and Mr. Hudson was directed to examine the hold, while Somers himself, with the marines and a couple of seamen, went to the cabin for the purpose of tracing the fugitive from his starting-point. This appeared to be no easy matter, for as yet there was not the slightest clew to his means of egress.

Somers opened the door of the state-room, which had been occupied by the prisoner, and there, to his utter astonishment and confusion, he saw Pillgrim, sitting on a stool, and looking as composed as though nothing had happened. Somers could hardly believe the evidence of his own eyes.

"Good morning, Mr. Somers," said the traitor. "I am happy to see you. I was just thinking it was about breakfast time."

"Haven't you had your breakfast yet?" asked Somers, who deemed it best to talk at random.

"How should I? You lock the door, and confine me to a very limited sphere of observation. I hope you don't intend to starve me."

"O, no, by no means. I thought it likely you had breakfasted while on your travels."

"On my travels?" said the prisoner, inquiringly.

"You have been out of your room."

"I?"

Pillgrim opened his eyes, and seemed to be astonished.

"Certainly you have. When we opened the door half

an hour since, you were not here. Perhaps you will not object to telling me where you have been."

"I have not been out of my state-room, as you must be aware."

"But you have," replied Somers, stoutly.

"Am I to infer that you accuse me of lying, Mr. Somers?" demanded the traitor, with an exhibition of dignity.

"I accuse you of nothing; I only say you have been out of your state-room."

"But I say I have not. I am your prisoner: it is hardly magnanimous to insult me in my present situation."

"Are you ready for your breakfast?" asked Somers, unwilling to pursue the conversation on that tack.

"A hungry man is always ready for his breakfast. My misfortunes have not impaired my appetite. I am ready for my breakfast."

Somers directed the steward to bring the prisoner his morning meal.

"Mr. Somers, may I beg the favor of half an hour's conversation with you, when I have done my breakfast?" added Pillgrim.

"It is hardly necessary."

"Excuse me; it is absolutely necessary for your comfort and safety as well as mine."

"Under such a threat, I shall certainly decline," replied Somers, coldly.

"I intended no threat. Send these people away, and I will speak."

"You may speak or be silent, as you please."

Somers stationed a marine at the door, and sent the others away, retiring himself to the farther end of the cabin. He was sorely puzzled to know how the prisoner had got out of his state-room, and why he had returned. He concluded that the opening of the hold had induced the latter step, but the former was still enveloped in mystery. He determined to give the prisoner another room, and make a more careful search in the one he now occupied.

When Pillgrim had done his breakfast, Somers called a couple of marines, and ordered them to put the prisoner in the aftermost room. The hasp and padlock were then transferred to the occupied room.

"Mr. Somers," said Pillgrim, as he was about to lock the door, "I should like to speak with you."

The tone was gentlemanly, and even supplicating, and Somers entered the room, closing the door behind him; but he was careful to cock his revolver as he did so, for the prisoner was a desperate man.

"I am ready to hear you."

"It is well you are."

"If you have any threats to make, I will not remain."

"Let me speak only the truth," said Pillgrim, as he looked at his watch. "In twenty minutes from now, we shall all be in kingdom come."

There was a malignant smile on the face of the traitor as he spoke, and it was plain to Somers that the villain did not speak without a cause.

"Somers, you have beaten me in the last game we played. I shall beat in the next one."

"I told you I did not come here to listen to threats."

"You will be a dead man in seventeen minutes, Somers," continued Pillgrim, glancing at his watch again. "I could not deny myself the satisfaction of informing you of the fact. But, Somers, you will have the pleasure of knowing that I shall share your fate."

"What do you mean, you villain?" demanded Somers, horrified by the thought suggested by the traitor's words.

"Gently, my dear fellow. Don't use hard words. But I am glad to see you are moved. Ah, Somers, I have you now," said the wretch, in mocking tones.

"Speak!" roared Somers, drawing his pistol.

"Shoot me, Somers. I will thank you if you will. It is better to be shot dead, than to be blown up, mangled, and then, after enduring a moment or an hour of agony, to be drowned. Fire, Somers!"

He restored the revolver to his belt, appalled by the terrible picture which the villain painted.

"Somers, I did leave my state-room. I was not willing to acknowledge it before your crew."

"How?"

"I have not time to explain. There are but ten minutes of life left to you and me. We will not waste them in what is of so little consequence to either of us. You know of what the cargo of the Ben Nevis is composed?"

"I do — of arms, ammunition, and provisions."

"Correct; the ammunition is stowed in the after part of the ship — under us, in fact. Captain Walmsley and myself have laid a train by which the vessel will be blown up when four bells strike. It wants five minutes of the time. Captain Walmsley is in a position where he can hear the bell," continued Pillgrim with perfect coolness.

"Marine," said Somers, opening the door.

"Here, sir," responded the man.

"Pass the word for the quartermaster to strike four bells, instantly," added the young commander. "I am ready. Mr. Pillgrim."

The traitor looked aghast.

CHAPTER XVI.

CAPTAIN WALMSLEY.

"MR. PILLGRIM, I am not to be intimidated by any such stuff," said Somers, when he had ordered the bells to be struck, which would produce the explosion.

"Perhaps Captain Walmsley will not think it best to fire the ammunition at the moment agreed upon; some discretion on this point was left with him; but I assure you, on my word and honor, that the train is laid which will blow up the Ben Nevis," said Pillgrim, earnestly.

"If you had not mentioned the name of Captain Walmsley, I might have believed you. As it is, I do not. Your word and honor do not weigh much with me."

"Don't insult me."

"I simply speak the truth. There! do you hear four bells?"

"I do; and if you are not blown up in half a minute, you may thank Captain Walmsley for his moderation."

"He is not villain enough to destroy the lives of forty men, his own people as well as mine, to gratify your malice and revenge. I give you *my* word and honor that he will do nothing of the kind."

Pillgrim looked hard at him, and seemed to be slightly disconcerted by the obstinacy of Somers.

"If he will not, I will!" said he, fiercely.

"I purpose to put you in irons, when you have said all you have to say."

"In irons, Somers!" exclaimed the traitor, springing to his feet, his face flushed with indignation.

"Since you are open enough to announce your intentions, it is plainly my duty to defeat them. Acknowledge that your plot to blow up the vessel is a mere scare, and I may spare you this indignity."

"You will find that it is a reality."

"Why don't it blow up, then?"

"It will, as soon as Captain Walmsley is ready. The Ben Nevis shall not again go into a Yankee port as a prize. Mark my words."

"Captain Somers," called Mr. Hudson.

"What is wanted?"

"The men in the hold report a smell of fire there."

"I will be with you soon," replied Somers, convinced by this message that there was some foundation for the threats of the traitor. "Go into the hold, Mr. Hudson, and find the fire, if there is any."

He was cool, and did not permit the wretch before him to see a muscle of his face move.

"There is fire there, Somers," said Pillgrim. "I know just where it is. In a few minutes it will reach the ammunition boxes."

"Corporal," said Somers, opening the door again.

"Here, sir."

"Put the prisoner in irons, hands and feet," continued Somers.

"Do you mean that, Mr. Somers?" asked Pillgrim, quivering with emotion.

"I do mean it, and I shall stand by till it is done."

"Will you leave me in the midst of the fire, ironed hand and foot?"

"I will. You kindled the fire; and if you perish by it, blame yourself."

Pillgrim attempted to resist the execution of the order, but the marines were resolute, and he was fully ironed in spite of his struggles.

"Now lock him in," said Somers.

"One word, Mr. Somers."

"Not another word;" and the young commander hastened from the state-room, and made his way to the scene of peril in the hold.

He did not believe that even Pillgrim was stupid enough to blow up the Ben Nevis for mere revenge; and Captain Walmsley certainly would do nothing of the kind, for he could have no strong feeling on the subject, at least not enough to sacrifice the lives of himself and his crew.

There was a smell of fire in the hold — the hold filled with powder, shells, and other combustibles. This fact tended to confirm the statement of the wretch; yet Somers was incredulous. When he reached the scene of danger he found the officers and the men timid about proceeding far into the hold, for if there was fire, there must soon be an explosion.

"Follow me, my men!" said he, as he walked aft on the cargo.

"Ay, ay, sir!" cheerfully responded the men, — for the American seaman will go anywhere an officer will lead him.

In the after part of the hold there was a dense smoke and a strong smell of fire.

"Keep back! You are all dead men!" shouted Captain Walmsley, as Somers advanced and discovered the speaker seated on a box.

"What are you doing here?" demanded Somers.

"I am going to blow up the steamer," replied the captain, who held in his hand a tin pan filled with burning oakum, chips, and other combustible material.

"Well, why don't you do it, then?" said Somers.

"For God's sake, Mr. Somers, don't stay here,' pleaded Mr Hudson.

"You needn't, if you are afraid," replied he, coolly.

"Mr. Somers, in one instant I can blow the Ben Nevis all to pieces," said Captain Walmsley, with a proper exhibition of tragic adjuncts.

"Why don't you do it, then?"

"I am willing to give you one chance to save your lives."

"You are very considerate. Mr. Pillgrim was going to blow her up for my special benefit."

"If you think I am not in earnest, you are greatly mistaken," continued the captain, as he stirred up the burning substances in the pan.

"I see you are in earnest, and I am waiting for you to blow her up."

"I will give you ten minutes to save your lives; for I have sworn this vessel shall never go into port as a prize. You and your people can take to the boats and save yourselves."

"Will you blow her up when we are gone?"

"I will."

"I have had quite enough of this, Captain Walmsley," said Somers, advancing to the fire king, revolver in hand. "Now go on deck, or I will blow your brains out, if you have any."

The captain looked at the revolver, and he might as well have acknowledged his defeat, for his face proclaimed it.

"If I should drop this into the cargo, it would blow up the ship."

"No, it wouldn't. There are nothing but solid shot and shell under you," replied Somers; and perhaps his coolness and self-possession were in a great measure due to his knowledge of this fact, for he had carefully inspected the cargo immediately after the capture of the vessel.

Captain Walmsley, with the blazing censer in his hand, made his way over the boxes, bales, and barrels which lay above the heavy articles, to the hatchway. The pan and its contents were thrown overboard, and the men informed that there was no danger. The captain was ordered into the cabin, where he was put in double irons, as his fellow-conspirator had been. He protested, at first, against this indignity. Then he begged, declaring that Mr. Pillgrim was the author of the plot by which it was intended to recapture the steamer. It was fully believed that Somers and his crew would abandon the vessel as soon as it was announced that there was fire in the hold, knowing that her cargo would readily explode.

Captain Walmsley declared that Pillgrim was a fool; if he had kept still till the fire was discovered, instead of declaiming over it beforehand, the plan would have succeeded. Somers doubted it; and when the humiliated captain was ironed, he was sent into his state-room, and a sentinel placed at his door. This business was hardly completed before the marine in charge of Pillgrim informed Somers that his prisoner wished to speak with him. The request was peremptorily refused.

"There, Mr. Hudson, I think we have fixed those fellows so that we shall know where to find them when we want them," said Somers, when the conspirators had been disposed of.

"Yes, sir; and if any other man had been in charge of this vessel, he would have lost her, Captain Somers. I should have voted for abandoning her as soon as I was satisfied that she was on fire."

"Perhaps I should, if I had not known the powder and shells were in the fore hold. But I did not believe the villains had pluck enough to blow themselves up for the sake of blowing me up. If there had been any real danger, they would have been the first to run away."

"Well, sir, I think you have managed them exceedingly well."

Somers was perfectly willing he should think so, and perhaps he thought so himself. At any rate, he was heartily rejoiced to get out of the scrape so easily, and fully resolved that the conspirators should have no further opportunity to exercise their talents at plotting on board the Ben Nevis.

There was a mystery still unsolved to the young officer, and with Mr. Hudson he repaired to the state-room in which Pillgrim had passed the night, — or ought to have passed it, — and commenced a further examination. There was nothing supernatural, or even very remarkable, in the absence of the prisoner, when the carpet was pulled up, and a square aperture, now closed by a pine board, was discovered in the corner of the room. In the ceiling there was a similar aperture, which had been filled up to correspond with the deck above. It was evident that a ventilator, which had been used to convey fresh air to the after hold, had been removed at some recent period.

As Captain Walmsley had indicated this state-room for the use of Pillgrim, it was probable that he had chosen it on account of this means of egress. Some time in the night he must have visited the prisoner, entering through this aperture, and conducted him to the hold below.

In the fine weather and smooth sea the Ben Nevis nearly made good the claim of the conspirators in regard to her speed, for all day she logged fifteen knots, and at three bells in the first dog watch Cape Henry was sighted, and at ten o'clock in the evening she anchored off Fortress Monroe.

By the first conveyance Mr. Hudson was sent to Washington with the despatches of Captain Cascabel, and one from Somers. On the second day the messenger returned, with orders from the department. The young officer took the bundle of documents into the cabin, and proceeded to examine those directed to himself. He was ordered to hand his prisoners over to the commandant of the fort, to deliver his vessel into the keeping of the senior naval officer on the station, and to rejoin his ship forthwith, taking passage in a supply steamer to sail on the following day. He was highly commended for the skill and energy with which he had discharged his duty on board the Ben Nevis, full particulars of which had been communicated by Mr. Hudson.

Another document contained his commission as master, the next rank above that of ensign, which had been solicited by Captain Cascabel. This paper was full of interest to the recipient of it, and he was obliged to open the long letters he had written to his mother and to Kate Portington, in order to add, in a postscript, this important intelligence. He was proud and happy, and more than ever satisfied that republics are not ungrateful, notwithstanding the tradition to the contrary.

At the proper time he proceeded to execute his orders in regard to the vessel and the prisoners. Pillgrim and his fellow-conspirator were brought on deck. The former looked easy and defiant, as usual, and assured his captor that he should be at liberty in a few days.

"Perhaps not," said Somers.

"You shall yet be cheated of your victim, but I shall not be cheated of mine," said he, with a malignant smile.

"I bear you no malice, Mr. Pillgrim."

"I do bear you malice; and the heaviest revenge that

ever fell on man shall fall on you before the end of this year."

"Your threats are idle. I have heard too many of them. Pass into the boat, if you please."

Pillgrim and Walmsley went over the side, and the boat pulled away. The chivalrous military officer removed the irons from their legs and arms as soon as he received them.

The Ben Nevis was to be sent to New York to be condemned, and Somers handed her over to the naval officer, according to his orders.

CHAPTER XVII.

OFF MOBILE BAY.

SOMERS was now entirely relieved from duty. He had delivered up the prize and handed the prisoners over to the proper officers. On the following day he went on shore to spend a few hours before the supply steamer sailed. On visiting the fortress, he received the astonishing intelligence that Mr. Pillgrim had escaped from the officer having him in charge, even before he had been placed in the casement appropriated to his use. Somers had cautioned the lieutenant to whom he had delivered him, of the danger of removing the irons, but his advice had not been heeded. The careless officer was now under arrest for his neglect of duty.

By none was this unfortunate event more deeply regretted than by him who had been the means of foiling the schemes of the traitor and handing him over to the custody of the government. Pillgrim had boasted that he would soon be at liberty. He was certainly a talented and a daring fellow; and to handle him safely, it was necessary to understand him thoroughly. Somers had a suspicion that the officer from whom the wretch escaped was bribed by his prisoner; but of course there could be no evidence on this interesting point.

A careful search had been made by the garrison of the fort, but without success. Pillgrim was dressed in the full uniform of a naval lieutenant, and in this garb his ingenuity would enable him to pass the military lines, if indeed he was not provided with the means of doing so by the faithless officer in charge of him. The prisoner had escaped on the preceding day, and there was now little hope of recapturing him; but Somers gave such information as he possessed in regard to the fugitive. Captain Walmsley had been less fortunate, and was still in durance.

The story of the traitor's escape was a very simple one. When the boat which had conveyed the prisoners from the steamer to the shore reached the pier, and they had landed, Walmsley began to protest against his confinement, being a British subject. He insisted upon seeing the commandant of the fortress; and while everybody was listening to this debate, Pillgrim slipped into the crowd and disappeared, passing the sentinels, who had no suspicion that he was a prisoner, without a challenge. Immediate search was made for him; but he must have taken to the water, since there was no other place of concealment which was not examined. A calker's stage was moored to the shore near the pier, and it was afterwards surmised that he had crawled under this, securing a position so that his head was out of water, and remained there till evening.

He was gone, and that was all it was necessary to know. The officer who had permitted him to escape would be court-martialed and broken, and that would be the end of it. At noon, as Somers was about to embark on the supply steamer, a letter was handed to him, which had been brought in by a contraband. The negro said it had been handed to him by " a gemman wid de anchors on his shoulders," whom he had met on the road to Williamsburg, nine miles from the fort.

The epistle was from Pillgrim, as Somers would have known from the writing, without the contraband's description of the person who had given it to him. He put it in his pocket, and did not open it till he had taken possession of his state-room on board the steamer. He was confident that it contained nothing but threats and abuse, and he felt but little interest in its contents. The writer, chagrined at the failure of his plot, was running over with evil thoughts and malicious purposes. Somers opened the letter and read as follows: —

OLD POINT COMFORT, July 14.

SOMERS: You have been promoted. You remind me of the fable. The goat went down into the well. The fox sprang upon his horns and leaped out. You are the fox; you jumped over my head; you went up; you are a master now. I congratulate you. You are the only man in the world I hate.

The Tallahassee is doing a good business for the South. She has captured fifty vessels. The Ben Nevis was her sister. You have her. There are more of the same family. You believe I am used up. No. I write this letter to inform you that I am not even singed yet, say nothing of being burned out. I shall be afloat soon. The Ben Lomond, twin sister of the Ben Nevis and the Tallahassee, will be at work in a fortnight. She will then be called the Tallapoosa. Look out for her.

The Ben Nevis was captured; my agents bought her again. The Ben Lomond is now at — you wish you knew where! I shall command her. I could not resist the temptation to inform you of my plan. I know you will enjoy my prospects!

You would like to make a little arrangement for the capture of the Ben Lomond. I wish you might. You will hear of her on the broad ocean in a few weeks, — capturing, burning, bonding Yankee ships. It will please you to read the papers then! I shall strike for a California steamer. Her treasure will make good my losses.

I am so anxious to meet you again that I am tempted to tell you where my ship is. I would like to meet you on her quarter deck. You are a remarkably enterprising fellow; perhaps we shall meet. If we do, I should feel justified in hanging you at the yard-arm. You belong to the South. You accepted a commission in her navy. You betrayed your trust. I shall *endeavor* to see you again.

Give my regards to the officers of the Chatauqua. Inform them of my present brilliant prospects. Remember me kindly to Kate Portington. Possibly she may be a little *chilly* when you see her again.

If you capture the Ben Lomond, otherwise the Tallapoosa, it would make you a lieutenant. Do it by all means.

PILLGRIM.

Somers read this singular letter three times before he could form an opinion whether or not its statements were mere idle boasts, and whether or not they had a foundation of truth. Was there any such vessel in existence as the Ben Lomond? This was the interesting and important question to him. At this time the Tallahassee was making fearful ravages among the shipping on the coast, and the success and impunity with which she carried on her depredations offered plenty of encouragement for the rebels to send forth similar vessels, if they could obtain them.

The Ben Nevis had been named after a mountain in Scotland; Ben Lomond was the name of another. The former was a Clyde-built vessel, and it would have been natural to give these twin names to twin steamers. Pillgrim, in the character of "Coles," had given him a certain amount of correct information in respect to the Ben Nevis, though he had deceived him in regard to her destination. He had obtained this knowledge by accident, and the Ben Nevis had been captured.

To Somers there appeared to be a strong probability that the statements contained in the letter were wholly or partially true. There were only two rebel ports into which it was possible for the Ben Lomond to have run — Mobile and Wilmington. The conspirators had told him that the Ben Nevis was bound to Mobile when she was actually going to Wilmington. Pillgrim, in his letter, declared that he was to command the Tallapoosa. If there was any plan at all, of course it had been laid before the Chatauqua sailed from Philadelphia.

Why did Pillgrim start for Mobile in the Chatauqua? Was it not possible that he intended, as second lieutenant of a national ship, to obtain the means of getting the Ben Lomond, or Tallapoosa, through the blockading fleet? Did he not endeavor to involve the fourth lieutenant in the meshes of the conspiracy for the purpose of obtaining his assistance in this work? It was plausible. Perhaps the recreant wretch had left some papers in his stateroom on board the Chatauqua, which would be intelligible in the light which he could bring to bear upon them.

Bewildered and astonished by the prospect before him, as he read the letter again and again, and considered its remarkable statements in connection with his previous knowledge, Somers spent the whole afternoon in his state-room, and was only aroused from his meditations by the supper bell. In the evening he resumed his study of the case, and tried to reconcile the theory he had framed with reason and common sense. There was nothing to conflict with this theory but the fact that Pillgrim himself had given him the information upon which it was based. The traitor would not intentionally betray himself. Perhaps he did not expect his statements would be credited; or if he did, he had twice before been equally reckless.

Then Somers attempted to analyze the mental constitution of Pillgrim. The conspirator seemed to be able to endure all misfortunes. The loss of the Ben Nevis had not affected him, and he had endangered, defeated his plan to recapture her by indulging in idle threats before the match was applied. He had been more desirous of mortifying, humiliating, and overwhelming Somers, than of recovering his lost steamer. With great talents for scheming and plotting, he had displayed the most amazing stupidity.

At this point the remark in the letter that Kate Portington would be *chilly* when he saw her again, came up for consideration. Pillgrim certainly had some purpose in view which was equal to, or greater than, his desire to serve the South, or even himself, in a pecuniary point of view. He was the friend of the commodore — had known the family before the war. Somers could not help believing that, in spite of his thirty-five years, he was an aspirant for the hand of Kate, and that the bond he had signed was for her use rather than his own.

Miss Portington might well be *chilly*, if she discovered that Somers had pledged a part of her fortune at the present stage of proceedings!

Somers was nervous and uneasy until he had reasoned and coaxed himself into a full belief in the theory which he had suggested. He could not wait for evidence, if, indeed, any could be obtained. For the present he was satisfied, and determined to proceed upon his hypothesis, just as though every point in the argument had been fully substantiated.

Our young officer was never idle when it was possible to work. If any of our readers believe that Somers was very "smart," very skilful, and very fortunate in his previous career, we beg to remind them, and to impress it upon their minds in the most forcible manner, that he owed more to his industry and perseverance than to the accidents of natural ability and favorable circumstances combined. For example, when he captured the Ben Nevis, instead of gaping idly about the deck, and thinking what a great man he was, he went into the hold, and made a careful examination of the steamer's cargo. The knowledge thus gained had prevented him from abandoning the vessel when she was believed to be on fire, and thus saved the prize and confounded the conspirators.

Somers was not idle now. He procured "Blunt's Coast Pilot," and "A Chart of the North Coast of the Gulf of Mexico, from St. Mark's to Galveston," of the captain of the steamer, and diligently studied up, and even committed to memory, the bearings, distances, and depths of water in Mobile Bay and vicinity. He carefully trained his mind on these matters so important to a seaman; and being blessed with a retentive memory, he hoped and expected to have this knowledge at command when it should be serviceable. It was hard study — the hardest and dryest kind of study; but he stuck to it as though it had been a bewitching novel.

To assist his design he drew maps and charts of the coast from memory, and was not satisfied till he could make a perfect diagram of the coast, shoals, islands, and bars, mark the prominent objects to be sighted from a vessel, and lay down the depth of water. He had nothing else to do on the passage; and as the steamer glided swiftly over the summer sea, he found it a more agreeable occupation than smoking, playing cards, and "spinning yarns," which were the employments of his fellow-passengers.

On the eighth day from Fortress Monroe the supply steamer reached the blockading fleet off Mobile Bay, and Somers was warmly welcomed by his brother officers.

Of course he had a long story to tell, which was listened to with interest. The escape of the late second lieutenant was received with becoming indignation. Somers was now the third lieutenant of the Chatauqua, and he moved into the state-room formerly occupied by Mr. Garboard, who had also advanced one grade in his relative rank.

"Somers, you are just in time for a big thing," said Mr. Hackleford. "Our Brave Old Salt is going to take us up Mobile Bay in a few days."

"Indeed?"

"Yes, the Old Salamander has issued his orders."

"God bless him!" ejaculated Somers, fervently, in much the same spirit that a loyal subject speaks of a popular monarch.

"Ay, God bless him!" replied the first lieutenant. "He is the ablest naval commander the world has yet produced. In my opinion he is the superior of Nelson, Collingwood, Decatur, Porter, Preble, and Hull. By the way, Mr. Somers, you were with him on the Mississippi?"

"Yes, sir; I was in the Harrisburg when the fleet passed Forts Jackson and St. Philip. But I am rather sorry the attack is to take place so soon."

"Why so?"

Then Somers showed him Pillgrim's letter; but as we intend to tell only what was done, not what was said, we will not record the conversation.

CHAPTER XVIII.

BRAVE OLD SALT.

THE most extensive and careful preparations were in progress for the events which, a few days later, astonished the world even more than the splendid achievements of the fleet below New Orleans. The squadron off the mouth of Mobile Bay had been actively employed for several days in sending down topmasts, superfluous spars, and rigging. Chain cables had been extended over the sides of the ships where the machinery was exposed to injury from the shot and shell of the fort. Chains and sand bags were placed on the decks where plunging shot might disable the engines. Boats were removed from the starboard to the port sides, for the fleet was to go in with Fort Morgan on the right, and close aboard of them.

The preparations were advancing when Somers reported on board of the Chatauqua, and of course he at once experienced the inspiration of coming events. If there was any man in the navy whom he admired and reverenced, that man was Admiral Farragut. It is true, he was not singular in this respect, for every man in the fleet was equally devoted to him. The "Old Salamander," who seemed never to be happier than when in the midst of the hottest fire which the engines of modern warfare could produce, was the idol of both officers and seamen. He was an honest, just, and humane man, one who involuntarily won the respect of every person with whom he came into contact.

We were never more thoroughly impressed by the honesty, justice, and humanity of a man, than when we took the hand of this "Brave Old Salt." His expressive eye, and his gentle, but dignified bearing, spoke more truly and forcibly of what he was, than the most elaborate biography which the pen of genius could produce. It almost passes belief that men can stand up and work and fight as officers and seamen worked and fought between Forts Jackson and St. Philip, and at Mobile Bay; but we can think of no better inspiration than the leadership of such a man as Admiral Farragut.

He was born in Tennessee — a southern state; his home was in Virginia — a southern state — at the breaking out of the rebellion. With all the motives which actuated Lee and Johnston, Tatnall and Hollins, to induce him to abandon the old flag under which he had fought in early youth, and served through all his manhood, he remained true to his country in the hour of her severest trial. Neither bribes nor threats could move him, and not for one instant did he falter in his devotion to the flag he had sworn to sustain against all foes. Glory, honor, and immortality in the hearts of his countrymen to the noble Admiral!

As a naval commander, he has no rival in the past or the present, in this or in any country. He has achieved, once, twice, thrice, what any board of naval officers that could have been convened from the boldest and most skilful naval heroes of the united nations, would have solemnly pronounced impossible. Chance might have given him the Lower Mississippi — it did not; but it could not have given him that and Mobile Bay, and the brilliant exploits up the Great River. Chance is capricious; it never metes out uniform success.

Admiral Farragut is not simply a brave and skilful seaman, for the stroke of genius shines out in all his battle plans, in all his preparations, and in all his movements, whether on the silent river, as his majestic ship leads in the van to the conflict, or under the most deadly and destructive fire that ever was rained down on a wooden hull. "Brave Old Salt" in the main rigging of the Hartford, as she breasted the storm of shot and shell from Fort Morgan, is a spectacle more sublime than can be presented in the annals of any other nation. The position he chose for himself on that momentous occasion, more truly indicates the key to his marvellous success than any other fact in connection with the battle. He was not there to expose himself needlessly to deadly peril; he was there to see and take advantage of the issues of the battle.

His position was a symbol of the intelligence and bravery which won the great battle. He saw with his own eyes — not with others; while his glorious personal devotion was a type for every other man, which was imitated from commodores down to powder-boys. We read of a general who could not remember where he was during one of the severest and most destructive fights of the war. If he had been in a position corresponding to that of the doughty old admiral, it would have been difficult for him to forget it. But personal bravery alone does not win the battle on the sea or the land. The admiral's victories are due even more to his genius — to his persevering industry in the elaboration of preparatory details.

"Brave Old Salt," as Somers always called him, was our young officer's beau-ideal of a naval commander. "Brave" he certainly was, and "Old Salt," to a sailor, means something more than a long experience at sea. It conveys to the nautical mind an idea of skill which no "lubber" can possess. It was bravery, seamanship, and those peculiar qualities which an "old salt" possesses, that made him great on the quarter deck, in command of a squadron.

Somers's admiration for the commander-in-chief of the

fleet off Mobile Bay was of no recent origin. Since he had first known him as "Flag Officer Farragut" at Ship Island, before the grade of Rear and Vice Admiral had been created in our navy, he had reverenced him as a superior man, and looked up to him with an almost superstitious awe. He could hardly realize that they were both of the same earthly mould, with the like human hopes and aspirations. Though, for a young man of his age, Somers regarded his rank of master as very high, it did not permit him to abate one jot or tittle of the distance which lay between him and the admiral. He did not feel any better entitled to tread the same deck with the glorious old hero, as a master, than he did as an ordinary seaman.

Somers returned to active duty as soon as he had reported to the first lieutenant of the Chatauqua, and he had the deck in the first dog watch on the day of his arrival. During the afternoon watch he had had plenty of time to report the incidents of his cruise in the Ben Nevis. Mr. Hackleford had immediately communicated to the captain the facts concerning Pillgrim's letter, and the recreant lieutenant's papers had been carefully overhauled in search of anything which would shed a ray of light upon the statements of the strange letter.

The only document which looked at all hopeful was a note written in cipher, to which there was no key among the papers. If the communication had been in Chinese or Chaldaic, there might have been a chance of unravelling it; as it was, the note was written in arbitrary characters, which were as cabalistic and unintelligible as the Egyptian hieroglyphics. Somers was annoyed and discomfited, for he had confidently reckoned upon finding some letter which contained a hint to guide him. There was nothing but this note in cipher.

To add to his chagrin, Mr. Hackleford was utterly sceptical in regard to Pillgrim's letter — did not believe the first word of it — called it "gas," and declared that it would be stupid and childish to pay the least attention to the document. Captain Cascabel fully concurred with him in this opinion, and both of them laughed at Somers for bestowing a second thought upon it.

"Nonsense! Mr. Somers!" exclaimed the first lieutenant. "There isn't a single scintillation of truth in the story. If there were even a glimmering of reality in the thing, I would look into it."

"But Mr. Pillgrim told me some truth in regard to the Ben Nevis," argued Somers.

"That is the best reason in the world for believing he has not done so in this instance," said Mr Hackleford.

"I suppose I must give up the idea, then."

"You must, indeed. If you don't, I am afraid your reputation for common sense and good judgment will suffer."

"Will you allow me to take this letter in cipher, and keep it till to-morrow?" asked Somers.

"Certainly."

Somers took the letter, and put it into his pocket until he had an opportunity to study its mystic characters. He was mortified by the rebuff he had received, but his faith, though somewhat shaken, was not destroyed. He was officer of the deck from four till six. Just before he was relieved, he ordered the side to be manned to receive the captain, who was just returning from a visit to the flag-ship.

As he touched his cap to Captain Cascabel, he noticed a smile on his commander's face, which seemed to relate to him, and he blushed beneath the pleasant, but expressive glance bestowed upon him.

"Mr. Somers," said the captain.

The officer of the deck stepped forward, and saluted the commander again.

"You are invited to dine with Admiral Farragut to-morrow afternoon."

"I, sir!" exclaimed Somers, completely overwhelmed by this remarkable declaration.

"Rear Admiral Farragut presents his compliments to Mr. Somers, and would be happy to see him at dinner to-morrow, on board the Hartford."

The captain passed on to the companion-way, leading to his cabin, leaving Somers as bewildered as though he had been invited to dine with Queen Victoria, Louis Napoleon, and the Emperor of Russia; indeed, he regarded it as a much greater honor to dine with "Brave Old

Salt," than to put his feet under the mahogany of the mightiest crowned head of the world. It was evident that somebody had been talking to the admiral about him; the captain and the first lieutenant of the Chatauqua certainly felt kindly enough towards him to do so.

To dine with Admiral Farragut! That was glory enough for a lifetime; or at least to be deemed worthy of such a distinction. Our friend Somers was no snob; he "looked up" to great people, especially to those who were really great. He pretended to no familiarity with his superiors, though some of the officers were dying with envy at the notice taken of him by the captain and first lieutenant of the ship. He did not assume to be familiar with men who had won a deathless fame in defending their country's cause. Perhaps there was not an officer in the fleet who would so highly appreciate such a compliment as that of which he was now the happy recipient.

When he was relieved from the deck, and went down into the ward-room, the news had gone before him, and the "idlers" there congratulated him upon his rising fame. But Somers broke away from them as soon as he could decently do so, and shut himself up in his state-room. He was actually dizzy at the idea of sitting down at the table with " Brave Old Salt" in the cabin of the Hartford; and though he took the cabalistic note of Mr. Pillgrim from his pocket, at least half an hour was wasted before he could apply his mind undividedly to the

17 *

difficult problem before him. Finally, the hope of making
a grand revelation to the admiral on the morrow fired his
zeal to such a pitch that the work looked like play to him.

Somers opened the mysterious document and spread it
out on the desk, at which he seated himself. It looked
dark and hopeless, with its dots and dashes, its horizontals and perpendiculars, its curves and crosses. We present the note in full, that our readers may be able to
appreciate the difficulty of the task he had undertaken.

If Somers had been a student of the occult sciences, he might have been more hopeful. An hour's hard study brought a gleam of light. He thought the note must be signed by Langdon. There were seven letters in the signature. This was his first ray of hope. He then placed all the letters of the alphabet in a column, and against each made the character that represented it in the cipher. Six letters were thus interpreted.

The next step was to place each of the letters thus discovered over its sign in the note. The second and third words of the epistle then stood, the eights being for undiscovered letters, as follows: 88nxlo8ond.

"Ben Lomond!" exclaimed Somers, as he gave a smart rap on the desk to indicate his joy at the discovery.

Three more letters were gained, and the oblique cross was only a mark to divide the words. The three letters before Ben Lomond must be, t h e. The solution began to be easy, though it required a long time to reach it. At midnight, when he was called to take the mid watch, he had it written out as follows : —

Washington, Twentieth of June.

The Ben Lomond is at Mobile, fitting out. Mallory gives you the command. The forts will be attacked by the first of August. You must get her out before that time.

LANGDON.

CHAPTER XIX.

THE BOAT EXPEDITION.

AT general quarters, on the following day, Somers looked somewhat care-worn. It was midnight when he had worked out the solution of the cipher, and at this hour he had been called to take the mid watch. But there was no happier or more exultant man in the fleet. His conquest over the cabalistic letter had confirmed his theory. The Ben Lomond was not a myth, and she was at Mobile. Pillgrim had expressed a desire to see Somers again, and there was a fair prospect that he might yet be able to do so.

The important event of this day was the dinner with "Brave Old Salt." But the letter and the dinner seemed to be inseparably connected. Somers had given the translation to the first lieutenant, who, to the chagrin and mortification of the persevering student, did not appear to attach much importance to the letter.

"If the Tallapoosa, or Ben Lomond, is in the bay, we shall soon have her," said Mr. Hackleford, "for we are going to make the attack on the forts within a few days."

"The attack may fail, and thus afford an opportunity for the cruiser to come out," suggested Somers.

"Fail?"

The third lieutenant of the Chatauqua stood abashed before the look of his superior. He did not believe that any attack made by Admiral Farragut could fail, but it was possible for the Confederate steamer to run the blockade, as hundreds had done before her, especially as she could steam sixteen knots.

"I don't think the attack will fail, sir; but even a victory might afford the Ben Lomond a chance to run out."

"I don't think there is much chance; but Captain Cascabel has your solution of the letter under consideration. Perhaps the admiral may have something to say about it."

Somers was not satisfied with the reception given to his revelation. He had already formed a plan for ascertaining where the Ben Lomond was, but the cool manner in which his communication was received prevented him from even mentioning it.

In the afternoon, the captain's gig came up to the accommodation ladder, and the commander, attended by Somers, seated himself in the stern-sheets. Captain Cascabel was received with due honors on the quarter deck of the Hartford, where the gallant admiral was walking at the time.

When his superior had been welcomed with dignified cordiality, Captain Cascabel introduced Somers. The admiral bowed, smiled pleasantly, and did not look patronizingly upon the young officer, as he might have been pardoned for doing. As he stood there on the quarter deck of the flag-ship, he was full of genuine dignity and true manliness — a noble representative of the American naval commander. He was of medium stature, well formed, and of elegant proportions. He seemed to be made of nerves and muscles, and when he moved there was an elastic spring to his frame, which impressed the observer with the idea of energy and vigor. He did not appear to stand on the deck, but to be poised independently in the air, resting on the planks beneath him more because it was the fashion to do so, than because he had any need of such support.

Somers removed his cap, made his best bow, and blushed like a summer rose. He was deeply impressed by the glance of the admiral, and the atmosphere around him seemed to be full of the man at whom he gazed in reverent admiration.

"Mr. Somers, I am happy to see you," said the admiral, in a tone so gentle and affable that it seemed to remove the "curse" of greatness far from him. "I have heard of you before, and I doubt not we shall be able to make you very useful to your country."

"Thank you, sir," replied Somers, not daring to say any more, and with the feeling of his childhood, that "boys ought to be seen, not heard."

The admiral, with this judicious commendation, turned to Captain Cascabel, and opened conversation with him, evidently determined not to spoil the young man by taking too much notice of him. Somers was soon at home with the officers of the Hartford, and behaved himself with becoming modesty and discretion. He dined with the admiral, several other officers of distinction being present. The conversation at the table, singularly enough, it may appear to our readers, did not relate to the war, or even to the navy. These topics appeared to be carefully excluded, though the reserve on this occasion was probably accidental.

Somers found sufficient pleasure in looking at and listening to the admiral, and the other distinguished officers, though he was not ignored, being kindly encouraged, by an occasional question, to use his voice. But he was not forward, and his very nature prevented him from indulging in any of that impudent familiarity which is so offensive to elderly men, especially if they occupy high positions.

After dinner, a matter of business came up, and it soon appeared that Captain Cascabel had given the admiral all the particulars relating to the Ben Lomond, including the letter in cipher, which Somers had interpreted. The conversation took place in private, with only the three persons present who were most intimately concerned. The letter was exhibited, and its solution explained.

"Mr. Somers, what is your plan? I am informed that you have one," said the admiral.

"I have one, sir, but I hardly hope it will merit your approbation," replied the third lieutenant of the Chatauqua.

"We will hear it, if you please. By the way, our picket boats report that a steamer came down the bay this morning, and moored inside the Middle Ground. It may be the one mentioned in your letter — the Tallapoosa."

"Probably it is, sir. She can now only be waiting the arrival of Lieutenant Pillgrim, who is to command her."

"We must capture that man. State your plan, Mr. Somers."

The young officer, with no little trepidation, related the particulars of the method he had considered for the capture of the Ben Lomond.

"Very daring and impudent, Mr. Somers," said the admiral, as he glanced with a meaning smile at Captain Cascabel.

"Mr. Somers's *forte* is daring and impudence. But his scheme, besides being based on mere theory, is absolutely fool-hardy," added the captain, throwing a whole bucket of cold water on the young officer's prospects.

"I do not wholly agree with you, captain. By the report of the picket boats, there is certainly a sea-going steamer in the bay. That, in a measure, confirms Mr. Somers's theory. Now, if the vessel is there, the young man may bring her out if he has the ability to do so. What force do you require, Mr. Somers?"

"The first cutter of the Chatauqua, and twenty-four men."

"You shall have them, Mr. Somers," said the admiral. "Instead of the first cutter, I suggest a whale-boat, which will not be much more than half as heavy."

"That would be better, sir," replied Somers, hardly able to conceal the joy and exultation he felt at the prospect of being permitted to carry out his plan.

"Captain, you will permit Mr. Somers to pick his men, and afford him every facility for the execution of his purpose."

"I will, with pleasure, sir."

"When do you wish to begin, Mr. Somers?" asked the admiral.

"To-night, sir."

"Very well. The monitors haven't arrived, captain, and it may be a fortnight before we make the attack on the forts. The steamer may run out in a fog or storm before that time, and I think we do well to prevent another Tuscaloosa from preying on the commerce of the country."

"Undoubtedly, sir, if we can."

"Mr. Somers's scheme may possibly succeed, though I

do not think his chances of cutting out the steamer
are very encouraging."

"I am afraid not, admiral," answered Captain Cascabel, incredulously.

"Mr. Somers, your reputation would be seriously
damaged by the failure of your enterprise. Your officers would be more unwilling to trust you than they are
now if you should meet with a disaster."

"I could not complain. I do not intend to meet with
any disaster. If I do nothing better, I shall bring my
men back with me."

The admiral laughed, and seemed to be pleased with
this confidence, while Captain Cascabel shook his head.

"Mr. Somers, the risk is very great. You and your
men may be prisoners in Fort Morgan within twenty-four hours. A failure would damage, if not ruin you.
Are you still ready to undertake the work?" asked the
admiral.

"I am, sir."

"Remember that everything depends upon yourself.
My best wishes for your success go with you."

Somers needed no better inspiration, and his frame
seemed to jerk and spring like that of Brave Old Salt,
when he realized that he was actually to undertake his
cherished purpose.

The gig pulled back to the Chatauqua, and Somers
immediately commenced his preparations. The cordial

indorsement of the admiral was enough to silence all opposition, and to "put a stopper on the jaw-tackle of all croakers." He was earnestly seconded by the captain and his officers. In a short time a light whale-boat was towed up, and made fast to the boom.

Somers's first duty was to select his crew. He was to engage in a desperate enterprise, and everything must depend upon the skill and bravery, as well as the silence and discretion, of his force. The first person selected was the boatswain, Tom Longstone, who, being better acquainted with the qualities of the seamen, was intrusted with the selection of the boat's crew. Just as soon as it was discovered that some daring enterprise was to be undertaken by the third lieutenant, he was beset by eager applicants for a place in the boat. Acting ensigns, masters' mates, midshipmen, indeed, all the officers below Somers in rank, begged to be appointed.

The young commander of the expedition was prudent and cautious, and he accepted the services of none. Tom Longstone was the only officer to accompany him. The boatswain would obey his orders without asking any questions, or bothering him with any advice.

"There, Mr. Somers, I have picked out the twenty-four best men in the ship — men that will work, fight, and hold their tongues," said Boatswain Longstone, when he had executed the important trust committed to him.

"Thank you, boatswain. What do you think of the weather?"

"It's going to be a nasty night."

"So much the better. Let every man take his pea-jacket; apply to the armorer for revolvers and cutlasses for each of them."

"A howitzer, Mr. Somers?"

"No; we must go as light as possible," replied Somers, as he proceeded to instruct the boatswain in regard to certain "slings" and other rigging that would be wanted.

Boatswain Longstone did not ask a single question about the nature or object of the enterprise; and with the exception of the admiral, and the captain and first lieutenant of the Chatauqua, not a man in the fleet besides Somers knew "what was up." It was necessary to conduct the enterprise with the utmost caution and secrecy.

The boatswain's predictions in regard to the weather proved to be entirely correct, for at eight bells, when the first watch was set, it was dark, foggy, and rainy. Somers had calculated upon this weather, when he had so promptly chosen the time for his venture. It was just the night for a difficult and dangerous enterprise, and the fog and the darkness were its best friends. While the boatswain was carrying out the orders given him, Somers had been engaged at the desk in his state-room, preparing for use certain papers, including his commander's commission in the **Confederate navy,** and his letter of instructions, intended for the Ben Nevis, or Louisiana. With his **knife** he scratched, and with his pen he wrote, until the documents suited his present purpose; and they were placed in his pocket.

At two bells — nine o'clock in the evening — while the rain poured down in torrents, Somers embarked with his force, consisting of **Tom** Longstone and twenty-four **as athletic and resolute fellows as ever pulled an oar or** handled a cutlass. The whale-boat was crowded, though it was of the largest size, being thirty **feet in length. The oars were carefully muffled, and the seamen were so disposed that the oarsmen could be** relieved without noise.

Wrapping his overcoat closely around him, Somers seated himself in the stern-sheets of the whale-boat, **with** the boatswain at his side. Though profoundly impressed by the magnitude and danger of the work **in** which he was engaged, he could not help thinking of the changes which had checkered his lot, since, two years before, he had sat in the first cutter of the Harrisburg, as an ordinary seaman. Now he was a master, and in command of the expedition. Tom **Longstone had been** with him **then;** he was with him now. In low tones, they talked of that eventful **night**, and of the changes which had occurred since that time.

Somers was grateful for his advancement, and thanked God that he had been enabled to perform his duty so as to merit the favor of his superiors. And in the depths of his heart he asked God to bless his present exertions for the good of his country. He leaned on the Good Father even in this exciting hour, and his religious faith was the strength of his arm.

CHAPTER XX.

THE PICKET BOAT.

THROUGH the deep darkness and the dense fog the boat made its way. There was not an object to be seen, on ship or shore, to guide its course; and in front of Somers there was a patent binnacle, whose lights were reflected on the compass, but did not even soften the gloom without, into which he continued to gaze with the most anxious solicitude. He had carefully estimated the currents the whale-boat would encounter, and calculated the force of the wind, so as to determine her lee-way with the nicest practicable accuracy.

The young commander of the expedition hoped to strike a certain point of the land to the eastward of the fort on Mobile Point, distant five and a half miles from the ship. Half a mile east or west of the desired point might involve him in serious if not fatal difficulties, and everything depended upon the accuracy of his calculations. His early experience as a boatman at Pinchbrook Harbor was of incalculable service to him, since nothing can supply the place of actual observation in the making of such nice estimates as were required for success in the present instance.

The rain poured down in torrents, and the sea was rough and uneasy; but Somers, never for an instant turned aside from the grand object before him by the discomforts of his situation, watched his compass and closely observed every motion of the whale-boat. He was fired with zeal, but he was not excited, for he knew how much depended upon cool judgment and careful execution of the details of his work.

"Breakers ahead!" said the bowman, in a low tone; and the words were passed aft to the officer.

Breakers were to be expected; and of course Somers was not appalled by the announcement. The boat dashed on till she reached the broken water; but the surf on the shore, thrown up by the storm, was absolutely fearful A stunning roar broke upon the ears of the young officer as the frail craft approached the foaming billows that shattered themselves on the beach.

"That's a heavy surf, Mr. Somers," said Tom Longstone.

"So much the better," replied the officer, cheerfully.

"This whale-boat will not be much better than a cockleshell in that surf."

"She will go through it, if she is well handled."

"Ay, ay, sir; of course she will."

"The rebels will not expect a boat to land in such a surf and on such a night. We shall not be expected," replied Somers, in a loud tone, for whispers and soft speech could not be heard above the roar of the billows.

The commander of the expedition stood up in the stern-sheets, and attempted to penetrate the gloom and fog in the direction of the beach; but neither sight nor sound of the shore could be obtained. To plunge through that boiling surf upon a rebel battery or an artillery company, would be a sad conclusion of the night's work; but even this must be risked, for it was not possible to obtain a single item of information in regard to the surroundings on shore.

"Oars!" shouted Somers, when he had completed his unsatisfactory survey shoreward, and there was not the slightest danger of his order being heard by an enemy beyond the thundering roll of the sea. "Hold water!"

The onward progress of the boat was stopped.

"Back the starboard, pull the port oars!" added the officer, who had now taken the management of the boat out of the hands of the coxswain. "Oars!" he continued, when the boat was turned so as to head directly from the shore.

"Now, my lads, pull steady, and mind the orders promptly." said the confident young officer. "There's a heavy surf; but if you pull strong, and mind quick, we shall be through it in a moment."

"Ay, ay, sir!" responded the blue-jackets.

"Stern, all!" continued Somers, when he had carefully observed the sweep of the last wave.

The oarsmen backed water, and the boat moved towards the shore, stern foremost. In a moment she was lifted up by a great billow and swept furiously towards the beach.

"Steady!" said Somers, gazing forward over the heads of the men, watching the approach of the next foam-crested wave.

The men were entirely cool, and their iron muscles held the boat under perfect control. A huge roller was coming in, fiercely, rapidly, at double or triple the speed of the whale-boat, and the first great peril of the surf was at hand.

The danger was, as our inexperienced readers may not understand, that the stern of the boat, suddenly struck by the swift-flying wave, would be lifted high in air, and the bow forced under; or that the boat would broach to, and be rolled over in the sea. In either case the boat would be swamped, and eventually be stove on the beach. Somers saw one of these rushing billows coming down with frightful velocity upon the whale-boat.

"Oars!" cried he; and the men ceased backing her.

"Give way!" he added, with an energy which was at once communicated to the muscles of the men: and they pulled steadily, as a well-disciplined crew always does, but with a firmness and strength which caused the boat to dart forward towards the savage roller.

She met the billow; her bow rose upon it; she passed over without being ingulfed by it.

"Oars! Hold water! Stern, all!" continued the young officer; and again the whale-boat moved towards the shore.

The manœuvre described was repeated several times, until the boat had passed through the surf, and struck heavily on the sandy beach. The men in the bow were then ordered to jump into the water; and as the forward part was thus lightened, the successive rollers bore the boat farther and farther upon the beach, until the whole crew were landed. The first step of the expedition had been safely accomplished.

Somers ordered the men to haul up the boat high and dry upon the beach. There was not a person to be seen, or a sound to be heard, which indicated the presence of an enemy. The young officer had now to prove the correctness of his calculations, for as yet he knew not upon what portion of the point he had landed. A careful survey of the ground was therefore immediately to be made. It was necessary to have assistance in this; and Somers selected two first-class firemen, very intelligent men, machinists and engineers, who were in training for situations in government ships. They had been brought to work the engine of the Ben Lomond, if, fortunately, she were captured.

Tom Longstone was left in charge of the boat and crew, and the two firemen followed the commander of the expedition, who moved towards the north. When he had proceeded a short distance, he explained to his companions his object.

"About an eighth of a mile from the beach," said he, "there is a creek, which widens into a little bay. I wish to find this creek; it will lead us into Mobile Bay. Conant, you will go east, and, Wade, you will go west. You must be very careful, or you will lose your way. You will not go more than half a mile, as nearly as you can judge, in either direction. If you find it, return to the beach, and take notice of the best way to reach it."

The firemen parted, and Somers moved forward himself. He did not find the creek in the direction he had chosen, and returned to the beach, after a search of about an hour. Wade was there before him; but Conant had not yet made his appearance, though he did not long delay the expedition.

"I have found it, sir," said Conant, when he returned. "It lies in this direction:" he pointed to the north-east. "It isn't a quarter of a mile distant; but I had some difficulty in finding a good path."

"Did you see anybody, or anything?"

"Nothing, sir."

The whale-boat was then turned over; each man took off his pea-jacket, rolled it up, and put it on his shoulder. The boat was then lifted up, and placed on the shoulders of the sailors, the garment acting as a cushion to support the weight, without injury to the bearers. After a great many trials and difficulties incident to the darkness of the night and the character of the ground, the creek was reached, and the whale-boat launched. Unfortunately, the water was very shallow, and even the light draught of the boat was too great for rapid progress, though by various expedients this obstacle was overcome, and the expedition reached the mouth of the creek at about half past twelve o'clock in the morning.

Somers was entirely dependent upon his memory and the compass for sailing directions; and the careful study he had made of the navigation of the bay enabled him to move with considerable confidence. The creek disembogued in a nearly landlocked bay, whose comparatively still waters were passed, and the boat began to be tossed by the waves of the broad bay.

Heading his craft to the westward, he bade the men give way with a will. Encouraged by the manner in which all obstacles had thus far been overcome, they were ready and willing subjects. After pulling about three miles, the rougher sea and the depth of water which the bowman had continually reported, assured Somers that he must have reached the Middle Ground, where vessels bound out usually came to anchor when subjected to any delay. The Ben Lomond, if she was in the bay, could not be far distant; but the fog and darkness prevented him from seeing a ship's length ahead.

"Can you see anything, Mr. Longstone?" asked the young commander, who felt that he was now in the midst of the greatest obstacles to the success of his mission.

"I can't see anything," replied the boatswain; "but I think I hear something. There, sir! Two bells just struck in a vessel dead ahead."

"I see her," said the bowman. "It's a rebel ironclad!"

"She's an ugly customer. I don't want anything of her," said Somers, as he ordered the boat to go about, and headed her to the north-east.

"Boat ahead, sir!" reported the bowman.

"Speak out, man!" said the commander. "I am not afraid of being seen now. Where away is she?"

"On the port quarter, sir."

"Starboard, coxswain," continued Somers.

In a few moments the dark outline of the boat was seen in the water, and the coxswain was directed to steer towards her. Somers was fully committed now, and intended to carry himself through by impudence and audacity. He was in the midst of the rebel fleet to be used for the defence of the bay. He knew that the waters around him were patrolled by picket boats, and he doubted not the craft before him was one of them. He could not find the Ben Lomond readily, and probably the officer of this boat would know her position.

"Boat ahoy!" he shouted.

"In the boat!" was the reply.

"Oars! Hold water!"

"What boat is that?" demanded the officer of the rebel party.

"My boat," replied Somers, rather irregularly.

"Who are you?"

"John Pillgrim, commander in the Confederate navy, appointed to the steamer Tallapoosa."

"Ah," responded the officer. "You were expected before."

"Couldn't come before," replied Somers, with perfect assurance. "Where is the Tallapoosa? I have been beating about here in the fog these two hours, trying to find her."

"She lies about half a mile to the northward and eastward."

"Thank you; I shall find her. Please report me to Admiral Buchanan, and say I shall run out immediately."

"It's a good night for it. I beg your pardon, Captain Pillgrim; have you a pass?"

"A what?" demanded Somers, as if astonished at the request.

"A pass."

"No; where should I get a pass, or what should I want one for?"

"Excuse me, but my orders are very strict. I cannot let a boat or vessel pass me without the proper papers."

"What papers do you want?"

"Simply a pass."

"I have no pass."

"I shall be obliged to detain you, then."

"No, you won't!" answered Somers, indignantly. "Here it is one o'clock in the morning. I ought to have been over the bar by this time."

"I can't help it, Captain Pillgrim; my orders are imperative," pleaded the picket officer.

"Well, if you can't help it, I can. I may not have such another night as this for a month."

"I shall not detain you half an hour. The Tallapoosa has steam up, and is only waiting for her commander and the balance of her crew."

"How many men has she on board?" asked Somers, somewhat startled.

"About forty, besides the firemen."

"I have the balance. It is all right."

"Pardon me, if I persist. I must see your papers."

"I have no pass; but I will show you my commission and my orders from the secretary of the navy."

"Those will answer."

The boat was laid alongside, and by the light of a lantern the officer glanced at Somers's commission and orders. He pronounced them all right, and the expedition was permitted to proceed.

19 *

CHAPTER XXI.

THE BEN LOMOND.

"THAT'S a bold step, Mr. Somers," said Tom Longstone, as the whale-boat dashed on towards the intended prize.

"If it were less bold, it would be more dangerous," replied Somers, easily; for he entered so fully into the spirit of the affair, that he felt quite at home, and was hardly disturbed by a doubt of final success.

"Where is Mr. Pillgrim now?" asked the boatswain.

"I haven't the least idea; but I think he cannot be far off."

"You left him at Fortress Monroe?"

"Yes; he had started for the South then, to take command, I suppose, of this vessel. The traitor's plan was to come down on the Chatauqua, and then bring out this vessel perhaps, on the pretence of capturing her. At any rate, he was going to use his official position in the navy to help him get the Tallapoosa out of the bay, and past the blockading squadron. If not, he would not have gone in her, and thus wasted so much of his valuable time. I wish I knew where he is now."

"Perhaps it don't make much difference."

"I am afraid it will make considerable difference. Suppose the traitor has been on board the Ben Lomond?"

"The what?"

"The Tallapoosa; they have changed her name. Keep a sharp lookout forward for the ship, bowman."

"Ay, ay, sir! I can't see a thing yet."

"Suppose he has been on board, Mr. Somers?" continued the boatswain.

"If he has, we may have to fight for the vessel."

"Well, we can do that," replied Tom, as he involuntarily grasped his cutlass.

"He has forty men aboard of her now, besides the firemen and coal-heavers."

"Our boys wouldn't mind forty of them."

"I should not hesitate to attack her, but the noise would wake up the rebel iron clads and gunboats. We must get the vessel without fighting. I don't believe Pillgrim has been on board of her. If he had, that picket officer would have known that I am not the man. I'm not going to croak about the business, though. In my opinion it will be all right."

"Of course the Tallapoosa is in charge of some one."

"All her officers are on board, except the commander, we were told."

"Some of them may know Mr. Pillgrim," suggested

the boatswain, who had more fears for his young commander than the latter had for himself.

"Mr. Pillgrim has been in the North, and in England since the war began. I am of the opinion that those on board do not know him."

"Suppose they do?"

"I shall put them under arrest if they refuse to obey my orders."

"You are smart, Mr. Somers," said Tom, who chuckled over the adroitness of his *protégé*, even while he trembled for his safety and success.

"Steamer ahead, sir!" reported the bowman.

"Where does she lie?"

"On the starboard bow, sir!"

"Port a little," said Somers. "Now, my men, you will obey orders and keep silent. Answer no questions which may be put to you."

"Ay, ay, sir," responded the crew, cheerfully; for though they seemed to be knocking at the door of a rebel prison, they had full confidence in their gallant young leader.

Perhaps some of them "had their doubts," for four and twenty men are hardly ever gathered together, among whom there are not more or less who are disposed to grumble, and croak, and imagine possible disasters. Within the rebel lines, surrounded by Confederate vessels, and on the point of confronting superior numbers, it would not have been surprising if these men had been rather uncertain of the future. Whatever doubts or fears they had, they believed in Somers.

"My lads," continued the commander of the expedition, in a low tone, "you are rebel sailors for an hour or so. You will talk and act as such. Do you understand me?"

"Ay, ay, sir."

"You will call me Captain Pillgrim."

The men had listened to the conversation between their officer and the pickets, and they comprehended enough of the plan to enable them to act intelligently.

"Tom," said Somers, "there is nothing to prevent me from acting just as Mr. Pillgrim would do, if he were in my place."

"That's so."

"I could go to sea in this steamer, and plunder all the vessels I could overhaul."

"So you could," replied the boatswain, who seemed to be amazed even at such a suggestion.

"I'm not sure that I am not carrying out the very plan which the traitor had in his mind. Perhaps he intended to do just what I have done, when he reached the blockading station."

"Very likely."

"Then I shall be Mr. Pillgrim, and carry out his purpose to the letter; only, when we get out of the bay I shall do rather differently from what he intended."

"Boat ahoy!" shouted a man at the gangway of the Ben Lomond.

"On board the Tallapoosa!" replied Somers.

"Keep off," said the man, who seemed to be the officer of the deck. "Who are you?"

"Commander John Pillgrim, Confederate States navy, and captain of this ship."

"Man the side, you lubbers!" added the boatswain, rather improving on the suggestion of Somers, given him at this moment.

"Captain Pillgrim?" said the officer of the deck.

"I said so. Is the ship ready to sail?"

"She is, sir; we have kept steam up all day, waiting for you."

"Good! You are the right officers for me. I commend you," replied Somers, as he mounted the accommodation ladder.

The pretended commander went up the side, closely followed by Longstone and a dozen of the sailors, and stepped down upon the deck.

"I have not the pleasure of your acquaintance, I believe," added Somers, confronting the officer.

"Mr. Swayne, second lieutenant, sir," replied the officer. "Mr. Langdon is below, sir. I will send for him."

Langdon! It was all up with Somers! Langdon knew him, had dined with him, had been intimate with him, and of course it would be useless to attempt to pass himself off as Mr. Pillgrim.

"Stop, sir!" said Somers, sternly, and with great presence of mind. "When did Mr. Langdon come on board?"

"Nearly a week ago, sir, when the rest of us did."

"Indeed!" added Somers, savagely. "Mr. Langdon and myself have a little account to settle. He has disobeyed my orders, and I never will go to sea with such a man as executive officer. Mr. Swayne, for the present you will act as first lieutenant. I shall put Mr. Langdon under arrest at once."

"Here he comes, sir."

"Mr. Longstone, you will arrest the first lieutenant at once; put him in irons if he resists," said Somers, as he saw Langdon come up the companion-way.

The stalwart boatswain confronted the astonished officer, as he approached the spot where Somers stood with the second lieutenant.

"By order of Captain Pillgrim, you are placed under arrest," said Tom, as, with a couple of seamen, he placed himself in front of the executive officer.

"Under arrest?"

"Yes, sir."

"What for?"

"For disobedience of orders."

"By whose command?" demanded the bewildered Langdon.

"Captain Pillgrim's, sir?"

"Impossible!"

"I beg your pardon, sir, but the captain told me to lose no time. He is going to sea at once."

"Is Captain Pillgrim on board?"

"Of course he is. I just came off with him. He ordered me to arrest you."

"Who are you, sir?"

"Blarney, sir!" exclaimed the boatswain, impatiently; "I can't stop —"

"Mr. Blarney, will you do me the favor to ask Captain Pillgrim for a moment's conversation with me. There must be some mistake, Mr. Blarney."

"Can't stop, sir," answered Tom, who could not even pause long enough to laugh at the rebel's blunder. "My orders are to put you in irons if you resist. What do you say, Mr. Langdon?"

"Of course I do not resist; but there is some mistake."

"No mistake, upon my honor. You may take my word for it, the business is all straight."

"With what am I charged?"

"With disobedience of orders; and, Mr. Langdon, you'll excuse me, but there's a suspicion that you mean to go over to the Yankees."

"I! To the Yankees!"

"Beg pardon, sir; but I can't stop to blarney any longer. My duty is plain; and I'll bet a month's pay you will see the captain sooner than you want to. Down below if you please, sir, to your state-room."

Langdon obeyed in dogged silence. No doubt he much wondered who the rough fellow was that subjected him to this summary treatment. But the salutary hint about irons seemed to satisfy him, and when he had gone into his room, the door was closed, and a seaman placed before it. Longstone returned to the deck, touched his cap politely to Somers, and reported his orders executed.

"Mr. Swayne, you will call all hands," said the new commander of the Tallapoosa, when his dangerous first lieutenant had been secured.

The boatswain of the steamer piped all hands, among whom the seamen from the Chatauqua mingled, and made themselves entirely at home.

"Mr. Swayne, will you do me the favor to read my commission to the crew," said Somers, handing him the document which he had carefully "tinkered" to suit the present occasion.

Tom Longstone held the lantern, and the acting first lieutenant promptly complied with the request of the assumed commander. The document proclaimed that John Pillgrim was duly invested with authority as a commander in the Confederate navy, and was duly signed by "S. R. Mallory," though whether that distinguished rebel functionary had actually issued the paper or not, Somers was himself as ignorant as the others who listened to the reading.

From his orders Somers then read enough to satisfy

any who might be in doubt of his appointment to the Tallapoosa, which name he had substituted for that of Ben Nevis, as it read on the original document, given him by Langdon, *alias* Lieutenant Wynkoop.

"Are you satisfied, Mr. Swayne?" asked the commander, when he had finished the document.

"Entirely so, Captain Pillgrim," replied the first lieutenant.

If he had not been satisfied, probably he would have been put under arrest as summarily as his superior had been a few moments before. With such an energetic captain, it was lucky for him he was satisfied! Perhaps Mr. Swayne was duly and properly impressed by the decided character of his commander, and deemed it prudent to raise no objections.

"Are you satisfied, gentlemen?" asked Somers, turning to the little group of officers.

Fortunately for them, and perhaps for Somers too, they were also satisfied.

"My lads," continued the courteous but decisive captain, "you have listened to my commission, and you have listened to my orders."

Somers paused, and the two first-class firemen from the Chatauqua started a demonstration of applause which was a complete success.

"My lads, I am going out to take a look at the Yankee fleet, to-night," he proceeded.

Applause.

"I am a fighting man."

More applause.

"That Yankee fleet will not stop me!" added Somers, with enthusiasm.

"That's so!" shouted one of the first-class firemen, who had a high appreciation of a good joke; and his remark was followed by a storm of applause.

"I repeat, my lads, the Yankee fleet will not stop me. I shall pay my respects to the Yankee admiral down there before the sun rises."

Tumultuous applause.

"Now, my lads, I mean just what I say, and I say just what I mean. I command this ship, and every man on board obeys me. I am going through the Yankee fleet; will you go with me?"

"Ay, ay, sir!" roared the crew; and the voices of the Chatauqua's people were prominent in the reply.

"Will you go where I lead you?"

"Ay, ay, sir."

"Very likely I shall send you upon the deck of the heaviest man-of-war in the Yankee squadron; but I will go with you."

"Bully for the captain!" shouted the enthusiastic first-class fireman, which remark was indorsed and approved by the crew in general.

"What an awful fellow he is! — a regular fire-eater," whispered Mr. Swayne to Tom Longstone.

"He will do all he says he will," replied the boatswain.

"Will he board a Yankee frigate?"

"It's like him; but he is as prudent as he is brave."

"Now, my lads, to your duty. We shall get under way at once, and I want every man to be true to God and his country," continued Somers.

"Three cheers for the captain!" shouted the fireman; and they were given with a will, as Somers walked aft.

CHAPTER XXII.

RUNNING THE BLOCKADE.

"MR. SWAYNE, you will get the ship under way at once," said Somers, as he turned from the crew, and walked aft.

The first lieutenant gave his orders, and the crew were soon walking round the capstan. The officers of the Tallapoosa had certainly used their time to advantage, for the crew was well disciplined, though the twenty-four petty officers and seamen from the Chatauqua were the spice of every movement.

"Where is the pilot, Mr. Swayne?" asked Somers.

"We have one on board, sir. He berths in the steerage. Shall I send for him, Captain Pillgrim?"

"If you please, do so."

A master's mate was ordered to find the pilot.

"Is he up to his business?" continued Somers, to whom the pilotage of the vessel was of the last importance.

"Yes, sir; he is the best pilot in these waters. He has taken out a great many vessels on worse nights than this."

"I could take the vessel out myself, so far as that is concerned," said Somers, nervously. "Does he know how to get through the obstructions?"

"O, yes, sir; he is perfectly familiar with everything about the bay."

"And the channel is full of those infernal torpedoes."

"It is, sir; but the pilot knows exactly where every one of them is located. We are in no danger from them; but they will blow the Yankee fleet sky high when they attempt to come up, as they probably will in a short time."

"So I understand."

"There will be fun here in a few days," added Mr. Swayne, rubbing his hands with delight, as he contemplated the destruction of the naval force gathered on the other side of the bar for the demonstration.

"The admiral down there is no joker," suggested Somers. "He won't feel his way, and then back out."

"It would be better for him if he did. Admiral Buchanan is his equal in every respect. With his ram he will stave in every wooden ship in the fleet. His monitors will be blown up on the torpedoes."

"I hope the affair will come out right," said Somers, rather indefinitely.

"It will; you may depend upon it, captain. Whoever is here when the thing is done will see the greatest smash-up that has happened since the war began."

"I hope so," replied Somers. "But suppose Admiral Farragut should run by the forts."

"He can't do it; the thing is utterly impossible. The torpedoes will sink his monitors — they are like lead, and if you shake them up a little, they will plump down on the bottom like a solid shot. His wooden vessels, even if he gets by the fort, — which can't be done, — would be all chawed up in half an hour by the ram Tennessee."

"Anchor apeak, sir!" shouted Boatswain Longstone, who was doing duty as second lieutenant.

"Captain Column, the pilot, sir," said the first lieutenant, presenting a person who had been waiting a moment at his side.

"I am happy to see you, Captain Column;" and Somers took his hand.

"Thank you, sir," replied the pilot, who was evidently astonished at the degree of intimacy with which the commander condescended to treat him.

Already the new captain had won a hard reputation abaft the mainmast. His stern and decisive measures with Langdon had been privately discussed among the officers, and it was the unanimous opinion that they had "caught a Tartar."

"Well, Captain Column, have you got your weather eye open? This is a dark and foggy night."

"Wide open, sir," replied the pilot, cheerfully; for

Somers's cordial greeting had already produced a good effect upon him. "The darker and foggier the better, captain, for such a job as this. But there are so many Yankee ships outside, you can hardly get clear of them without a shot or two."

"O, I don't mind that, if you can get us well over the torpedoes, and through the obstructions."

"The obstructions are not of much account, and as for the torpedoes, I could put my hand on every one of them with my eyes shut."

"Good; but I don't want you to put your hand or my ship on them."

"Certainly not, captain," laughed the pilot. "I know how to keep clear of them."

"That will suit me better. The ship is in your hands, Captain Column."

A quartermaster from the Chatauqua was placed at the wheel, and when the anchor was heaved up, the Tallapoosa started on her course. Her wheels began to turn very slowly at first, and before she had gathered any headway, a boat touched at her side.

"Boat alongside, Captain Pillgrim," reported Mr. Swayne.

"What boat?"

"I don't know, sir."

"I have no more time to waste; keep the ship moving."

As the Tallapoosa gathered headway, a gentleman, clothed in naval uniform, stepped on the rail from the accommodation ladder. When he had reached this point, he stopped and looked down at the boat.

"Stop the steamer!" shouted he, in tones of authority; and to those who had heard it before there was no mistaking that voice.

It was Pillgrim, without a doubt! Somers was vexed and disappointed at this accident, which threatened to overthrow all his plans; but he promptly decided to treat him as he had Langdon.

"See what he wants," said the commander to Swayne, "but don't let the ship be delayed a single instant."

"Stop the steamer!" shouted Pillgrim, with a volley of oaths, because his first order had not been heeded. "Stop the steamer, or you will swamp my gig!"

"Your business, sir, if you please," said Swayne, stepping up to him.

"Don't you hear what I say?" replied Pillgrim, angrily. "Stop the steamer."

"It can't be done, sir."

"Can't be done!" gasped the traitor. "It can and shall be done."

"Who are you, sir, that step upon this deck in thy overbearing manner?" demanded the first lieutenant, roused by the tones and the manner of the new comer

"I'll let you know who I am. Where is Langdon?"

"None of your business where he is," said Swayne, spunkily. "What do you want here!"

"You shall soon know what I want here?"

Pillgrim was boiling over with passion at the rough reception given him by his officers on board his own ship. He was disposed to be even more stern and severe in his discipline than Somers had been.

"Who are you?" demanded Swayne.

"None of your business who I am, if you don't know; but I will soon bring you to your senses," roared Pillgrim, as he leaped down upon the deck, and with the step of a conqueror moved aft towards the wheel.

"Halt, sir!" said Mr. Swayne, placing himself in front of the stranger; for he was roused to a high pitch of anger and excitement by the unwarrantable conduct of the interloper. "You can go no farther on this deck, sir, till you explain who and what you are."

Somers stood where he could see without being seen; for his presence on the deck of the Ben Lomond would have explained to Pillgrim the reason for his uncourteous reception. He quietly sent the two firemen and a couple of seamen to the assistance of Mr. Swayne.

"I am the captain of this ship," replied Pillgrim, who found it necessary to make this statement.

"The man is crazy," muttered Swayne.

"You understand me now," growled Pillgrim. "Stop the ship!"

"I think not, sir," replied Swayne, coolly; and he evidently regarded the claim of the stranger in the light of a joke, or as the whim of a maniac.

"You think not!" gasped Pillgrim, roused almost to madness by this cool disregard of his authority. "I'll have you in irons in three minutes, you scoundrel."

"There, sir, I have heard enough of this!" said Swayne. "No man uses such language as that to me with impunity."

"I tell you I am the commander of this steamer," added Pillgrim, who doubtless felt that the epithet he had used was unbecoming an officer and a gentleman.

"I don't care what you are. If your boat is alongside, you will go into it, in double quick time."

Pillgrim began to storm again, shouted to the pilot to stop the steamer, and behaved in the most violent manner. Mr. Swayne's patience was totally exhausted, and he ordered the seamen who stood near him to arrest the interloper. A sharp struggle ensued, in which Pillgrim was overpowered, and was held fast by the stout tars of the Chatauqua.

The first lieutenant then explained to the captain what had passed, and what he had done.

"Put him in irons!" said Somers, decidedly.

"Who is he, captain?"

"It matters not who he is. No man can behave in that manner on board of this ship."

Swayne executed his orders to the letter, and the traitor, in spite of his struggles, in spite of his explanations and appeals, was put in irons on the quarter deck of his own ship. He was carried below, and put in a state-room, which was guarded by Conant, who had orders to shoot him if he did not keep quiet.

In the mean time, the Ben Lomond, — for Somers, in strict accordance with the subsequent "ruling" of Mr. Seward, refused to recognize the vessel by any other than her original name, calling her the Tallapoosa only in the presence of the rebels, — the Ben Lomond, under the skilful guidance of the pilot, was slowly making her way out of the bay. A quartermaster had been stationed in the fore-chains when the steamer got under way, to take the soundings, which seemed to be the pilot's principal reliance in the difficult duty he had undertaken. Captain Column had placed himself on the port rail, just abaft the foremast, and the steering directions were sent aft through a line of officers to the helmsman.

"By the deep four," sang the quartermaster in the chains.

"Steady!" said the pilot. "Keep her sou'-west by west, half west."

"Steady!" responded the quartermaster at the wheel. "Sou'-west by west, half west."

"By the mark five!" said the leadsman, a little later.

"We are getting into deep water," said Somers.

"Yes, sir; we shall deepen till we get seven fathoms."

"And a half five!" came from the chains. "By the deep six."

The pilot went on the bridge, and taking the cord attached to the whistle of the engine, made a signal, consisting of several blasts, with irregular intervals between them. A heavy bell on shore sounded several times in answer to the signal.

"All right," said the pilot. "I know exactly where I am."

"By the deep six!" called the leadsman.

The pilot repeated the signal with the whistle, which was answered from the shore by the bell.

"Quarter less seven!"

"It is all going right, captain," said the pilot to Somers, who stood on the bridge with him.

"By the mark seven!"

"Hard a port!" shouted the pilot, as he gazed into the binnacle on the bridge.

"Hard a port!" repeated the line of officers, till the order was returned by the wheelman.

"Steady!" said the pilot.

"Mark under water seven!" cried the quartermaster in the chains.

"Keep her south by west," added the pilot.

"South by west!" returned the wheelman.

"This course will bring us into the midst of the Yankee fleet in about twenty minutes," said Captain Column.

"I'm not at all afraid of the Yankee fleet," replied Somers.

"I'm not afraid of anything else," laughed the pilot.

"Where are the torpedoes?"

"Between us and Fort Morgan, which is only about a third of a mile distant, on our beam."

"And the obstructions?"

"We have passed them; they are of no account. Captain, I think all your troubles are yet to come," said the pilot, as he glanced ahead.

"Why so?"

"If we should happen to plump into one of those monitors, a fifteen inch shot would finish this craft in less time than it would take to read a man's epitaph."

"I have prepared for all such accidents. The Yankees will not fire on me."

"No?" exclaimed the pilot, wonderingly.

"I think you don't know me."

"I heard the first lieutenant say you were coming down here in one of the Yankee ships."

"I did."

"Did you, though?"

"We will come to anchor, pilot, when we get within hail of the Yankee squadron."

"Come to anchor, sir?"

"Certainly; come to anchor, until the fog clears off, or we can get a little daylight. I don't want much."

"Well, that beats me!" ejaculated Captain Column.

"I shall hoist the Yankee flag over the Confederate; then the Yankees will think this ship is a prize, and will not fire into her."

"That beats me!" repeated the pilot.

"I came down here in a Yankee man-of-war, and I made the arrangements for carrying this thing through before I left her."

"O, yes, I see!" laughed Captain Column. "You are playing them a Yankee trick."

"Exactly so!"

"Capital! capital!" exclaimed the pilot.

Fifteen minutes later, the Ben Lomond came to anchor under the lee of Sand Island, to wait for a favorable time to continue her voyage.

CHAPTER XXIII.

A YANKEE TRICK.

THE rebel officers and crew of the Ben Lomond were greatly astonished when the order was given to let go the anchor. They were not in a condition to appreciate the policy of stopping the wheels, and waiting for daylight within hail of the blockading squadron, reënforced as it had been for the attack on the forts; but as the captain had the reputation of being a perfect tiger, a fire-eater of the most ravenous sort, they did not venture to grumble or make any complaints.

Captain Column, the pilot, chuckled, and declared it was all right; the commander knew what he was about, and would get the steamer out of the scrape without even a shot from the Yankee men-of-war.

Somers had kept up his dignity and maintained his self-possession in the exciting scenes through which he had just passed; but it must not be thought that he was as easy in mind as he appeared to be. Every moment had been burdened with its own peculiar anxiety. The least slip, the slightest accident, would expose him and his brave followers to great peril, if not to capture and death. He had won the day thus far by the mere force of impudence and self-possession; but it was not without a fear of failure, disgrace, and captivity.

But everything, up to this time, had worked admirably. He had met and successfully turned aside the obstacles which beset him; and when the Ben Lomond came to anchor, the prospect looked more hopeful than at any previous hour. It was now about two o'clock in the morning. As there was nothing to do, he devoted an hour to an examination of the vessel, which had been fitted up at Mobile as a rebel cruiser. She had a heavy rifled pivot gun amidships, and four broadside guns, and was in every respect well provided for the work in which she was to engage.

She was a vessel of about four hundred tons measurement, long, narrow, and very sharp. Her rig was that of a topsail schooner, and her smoke-stack raked with her masts. She was a beautiful craft, and no labor or expense had been spared to make her the fastest and most elegant vessel afloat.

Even in the darkness, Somers could see enough of her shape and fittings to excite his admiration. He passed from the spar deck to the berth deck, where everything was in keeping with her appearance above. The wardroom was small, but it was comfortable and well arranged, and the captain's cabin was fitted up like that of a royal yacht. Probably Mr. Pillgrim had spent some of his own money on these arrangements before she left the Clyde; but what contributed distinctly to make her a war steamer had been done after her arrival at Mobile.

Somers was delighted with the arrangements of the prize, and as he examined the commander's cabin, he could not help envying the man who was permitted to occupy this sumptuous and convenient apartment; that is, if the stars and stripes floated at the peak above him, for he would rather have been a coal-heaver in a loyal ship, than in command of the Ben Lomond under the flag of the Confederacy.

Mr. Swayne had conducted Somers over the vessel, and pointed out to him those features which were most worthy of notice.

"She is a splendid vessel," said the young commander, as they paused in the ward-room.

"Yes, sir; I am but too happy in being appointed to such a ship. If we only get clear of the Yankee squadron, we shall give a good account of her."

"We shall have no quarrel with the Yankee ships," replied Somers, as he led the way to the spar deck again, for he was not disposed, just yet, to let Pillgrim and Langdon, who were confined there, hear his voice.

"Captain Pillgrim, you seem to be more confident on this point than your officers," replied Swayne, in a gentle tone, which more than insinuated that he would like to know more of the commander's plans.

Somers was very anxious that he should know more of them, so as to prevent any suspicions which his subsequent course might excite.

"From what point did you expect me to come, before my arrival?" asked Somers.

"I had no idea. Mr. Langdon seemed to be familiar with all your movements, but he did not say much about them. He did remark, at one time, that you were coming down as second lieutenant of one of the Yankee men-of-war."

"Did he, indeed? Well, he was a prudent man, and he will have his reward within a few days. Did he really say that?"

"He did."

"I was deceived in him; he was not to be trusted. I placed every confidence in him. What else did he tell you?" asked Somers, artfully.

"Nothing else, sir. He said more to me than to any other officer, and hardly anything to me."

"He has betrayed me."

"He told only me that you were to come in a Yankee man-of-war."

"Yes, he did; the pilot knew it — spoke to me of it; and very likely every man in the ship has the news. But, Mr. Swayne, the statement was true."

"Mr. Langdon afterwards contradicted it, and said you were in Richmond, and were coming down by land."

"Probably he thought he had made a blunder. I did come down in the Yankee ship, the Chatauqua. I am third lieutenant of her, not second. I was sent off by the captain, at my own suggestion, of course, to bring out this vessel. I have done it — haven't I?"

"You have," laughed Swayne. "Then you are expected by the Yankees?"

"Of course I am."

The first lieutenant of the Ben Lomond indulged in a laugh highly complimentary to the skill and cleverness of his commander. Somers laughed with him. It was an excellent joke to both parties, though, like the Druid shield, it was seen from different points of view.

"Capital!" exclaimed Mr. Swayne, when he had evaporated the foam of his mirth.

"If the fog clears off, I shall let up some rockets, which will prevent the Yankees from firing at us. You understand?"

"I see, sir: you have the Yankee signals?" chuckled Mr. Swayne.

"Every one of them. No doubt they are on the lookout for me in every ship in the squadron."

"Excellent, Captain Pillgrim. This is, by all odds, the best joke of the season."

"Now, Mr. Swayne, you will hoist the Yankee flag over the Confederate."

"I don't like to do that, captain," added Mr. Swayne, with a burst of patriotic enthusiasm.

"For a purpose, Mr. Swayne. Of course, when the men-of-war see that flag over the other, they will not fire. We shall run through the squadron, as though we belonged to it; and then — well, you will see what you will see."

"Exactly so!" exclaimed Mr. Swayne, who seemed to enjoy the prospect exceedingly, even independent of his desire to flatter and "toady" to his commander.

The flags were hoisted as Somers directed, and the "captain" for a couple of hours planked the deck in silence, impatiently waiting for the fog to lift, or for the daylight to come. It was his policy to anchor, because he was fearful that the steamer would run by the squadron, in the fog and darkness, and it would excite suspicion to return to the fleet, after safely passing through it. If Mr. Swayne had suspected any treachery, or that everything was not as it appeared to be, it would have gone hard with Somers and his men, for he could call in double the loyal force to assist him, besides releasing Pillgrim and Langdon.

At four o'clock in the morning, the fog lifted, and Somers directed the rockets to be discharged, and the steamer to be got under way. Though anxious to keep up appearances, he quietly directed Tom Longstone to make as much delay as possible, and by some accident the messenger parted when the anchor was apeak, and it was necessary to do the work over again.

"Captain Pillgrim, what shall be done with the men who came on board with you?" asked Mr. Swayne, while the crew were walking round the capstan.

"What shall be done with them?" asked Somers, apparently not comprehending the meaning of the question.

"They are Yankees — are they not?"

"They are true men, Mr. Swayne. I selected them for this very duty, and I know them."

"Excuse me, sir, I heard one of them singing a Yankee song, just now."

"They have been in the habit of singing such songs lately; but they are true men, and will stand by me to the last. If I had wanted them, I might have brought off a hundred of the crew of the Chatauqua."

Somers told a great many truths in the course of the night, for the purpose of deceiving the enemies of his country, which is a very anomalous duty for truth to perform.

The anchor was at the hawse hole, was "catted and fished;" and the Ben Lomond moved on again, with the pilot on the bridge. As the fog lifted, and the daylight increased, the squadron of "Brave Old Salt" was seen by Somers and his companions. As he had promised, not a ship fired on the steamer, or offered to molest her. The first lieutenant, pilot, and other officers were entirely satisfied that everything was working in exact accordance with the plans of their "smart" commander, as they already called him.

The exciting moment when all the delusion would be swept away, and the rebel officers and seamen find themselves prisoners, and their ship a prize, was at hand. Somers had already arranged his final movements with the boatswain, and certain of the men were instructed to perform particular parts in the closing scene of the drama.

"Now, Captain Column," said Somers to the pilot, "we must run down for the Chatauqua. She is the last vessel in the squadron, and if we appear to be moving towards her, nothing will be suspected."

"Exactly so, captain," replied the pilot, shaking his fat sides with laughter at the Yankee trick which they were playing off upon the originators of this species of pleasantry.

"It is quite smooth this morning. The wind has all gone down. Run right under the quarter of the Chatauqua."

"I can take her within six feet of the ship, if you like."

"Not too close."

"They will give us three cheers, won't they?" laughed the pilot.

"Very likely."

"Port!" shouted the pilot, as the Ben Lomond approached the Chatauqua.

"Port!" yelled the quartermaster at the helm, at whose side stood Tom Longstone.

"Port!" repeated the pilot with greater energy, when he saw that the head of the steamer was swinging off from the Chatauqua.

"Port!" again responded the quartermaster.

"Starboard a little more," said Tom, in a low tone.

Captain Column began to storm because the helm did not go to port as he ordered.

"Can't help it, sir. The tiller chains are jammed, sir," replied the quartermaster.

"Now hard a port!" said Tom Longstone.

"Starboard! Hard a starboard!" screamed the pilot, in tones of fury.

"Helm is jammed, sir!" returned the boatswain.

At this moment the bells were rung to stop, and then to back the engine. To all but the half dozen loyal seamen who stood near the helm, everything seemed to be in confusion. The Ben Lomond ran up on the lee side of the Chatauqua, and stopped within a few feet of her. A stroke of the wheels and a turn of the helm brought her alongside, before the rebels could clearly apprehend the situation. The twenty-four men, with their revolvers and cutlasses, stood ready to check any demonstration on the part of officers or crew, but none was made. Their weapons were in the armory, and they suspected nothing till an instant before the steamer touched the ship's side.

Conant, as instructed, leaped on board the Chatauqua, and reported Somers's wish to the officer of the deck.

In another moment, the watch on deck of the man-of-war poured into the prize, and secured every officer and seaman. Then came the three rousing cheers which the pilot had expected, and the work was done.

If ever a rebel was disappointed, disheartened, and disgusted, it was Mr. Swayne. He had been bewildered by the sudden change in the course of the steamer, and actually believed that it was caused by the wheel chains being jammed, until the watch from the Chatauqua poured in upon her decks.

"Well, Mr. Swayne, I suppose you are satisfied that I spoke the truth. The Yankees have not fired upon us; I came down in the Chatauqua; I was sent off to bring out this vessel; I have done it," said Somers.

"I had no suspicion you were a Yankee," replied the first lieutenant. "Where did you get your commission?"

"It was given me by Mr. Langdon and Mr. Pillgrim, both of whom are under guard below."

Swayne used some expletives more forcible than polite, and Somers went on board the Chatauqua to report.

CHAPTER XXIV.

PILLGRIM AND LANGDON.

"I HAVE the honor to report the capture of the Ben Lomond, otherwise the Tallapoosa," said Somers, as he advanced towards Mr. Hackleford, his face red with blushes, and his heart bounding with emotion.

The first lieutenant of the Chatauqua had regarded his enterprise with a want of faith, to say the least; and when the young commander of the expedition came forward to report its entire success, there was something like pride and exultation in his manner, mingling not ungracefully with the manifestations of his natural modesty. He had done "a big thing;" he felt that he had done "a big thing;" and it would have been a ridiculous affectation for him to pretend, by word or manner, that he had not done "a big thing."

"I congratulate you upon your success, Mr. Somers," replied Mr. Hackleford, warmly. "I was sceptical, I confess; but no man in the fleet is happier than I am at your good fortune."

"Thank you, sir," said Somers, blushing more deeply than before, and almost wishing that the first lieutenant had done the "big thing" instead of himself, because he was so kind and generous in his commendation.

"You have managed the affair with skill and energy. For my own part, I did not believe you would even get into the bay, let alone capturing the vessel. I am astonished at your success, but none the less delighted because I am surprised."

"Thank you, sir," was all Somers could say in reply to this praise so magnanimously bestowed.

"Captain Cascabel will see you, in his cabin, and we will hear your verbal report there."

Mr. Garboard had already gone on board the prize, hauled her off from the ship, where she was chafing her sides, and moored her a cable's length distant. Somers went below, where he was as warmly and generously greeted by the captain as he had been by the first lieutenant. He related the story of his night's adventures to them with all necessary minuteness. His auditors could not help laughing when he told them what he had done with his old friends, the first lieutenant and the commander of the rebel craft. He had acted on his theory of Pillgrim's intended movements, and thus kept himself above suspicion.

"How does Mr. Pillgrim appear?" asked the captain.

"I haven't seen him, sir; I was very careful not to

let him see me. Mr. Swayne, the first lieutenant of the Ben Lomond, after I had disposed of Langdon, managed him for me."

"It's a very amusing as well as a very exciting affair. But we must see these officers. Where are they?"

"Under guard in the state-rooms of the prize, sir."

"Bring them on board, if you please, Mr. Somers. Get your breakfast first."

Somers went to the ward-room, where he breakfasted with the officers off duty. He was cordially congratulated upon his success, though perhaps some of the mess regarded him as rather exclusive in permitting none of them to share his laurels.

After breakfast the first cutter was cleared away, and Somers pulled to the prize in her. The Ben Lomond was temporarily in charge of the second lieutenant of the Chatauqua, who had secured the prisoners, and put everything in order on board. Somers went at once to the ward-room, where the two most important prisoners were confined. There were now at each door a couple of marines with loaded muskets, but no communication had been had with the solitary occupant of either.

Pillgrim had several times attempted to obtain some information in regard to what was going on, but he was still in darkness. Even the bull's eye in his room could not have enlightened him, for it was on the starboard side of the steamer, while the Chatauqua lay on the port side.

Somers ordered the marines to open the door of Langdon's room first, and the late first lieutenant of the Tallapoosa came forth.

"Lieutenant Wynkoop, I believe," said Somers, facetiously.

Langdon looked at him with astonishment.

"Have you any more old sherry that has made two voyages to India?"

"This is hardly magnanimous, Mr. Somers," said Langdon, coldly.

"Perhaps not; but when officers stoop to such tricks as those you have practised, there can be no great harm in mentioning them."

"Mr. Somers, I find myself somewhat bewildered."

"I dare say," laughed Somers. "Very likely your friend Pillgrim, or Coles, is in the same situation."

"Is he on board?"

"He is."

"I have not seen him since he left Philadelphia in the Chatauqua."

"I have."

"You were in the Chatauqua with him?"

"For a short time."

"I had a letter from him, dated at Richmond, saying that he had changed his plans."

"Changed them — did he?" said Somers, who had

changed them for him. "Perhaps you will inform me how you happened to be on board this vessel."

"I don't object; it makes little difference what I say now. After obtaining the command of the Tallapoosa for Pillgrim, I went to Wilmington, where I was to take command of the Coosa."

"You mean the Ben Nevis."

"I do."

"I thought you were to call her the Louisiana."

"We did not always give you correct information," added Langdon, with a sickly smile.

"Go on."

"While at Wilmington I got a letter from Pillgrim, then in Richmond, informing me that the Ben Nevis had been captured, and that I was appointed first lieutenant of the Tallapoosa, if I chose to take the place. I did choose to take it, hoping soon to be in command of one of the California steamers. I went to Mobile at once, and attended to the fitting out of the ship. Pillgrim wrote me that he should be on board by the 22d, and I had steam up to run out the moment he arrived."

"How happened you to tell your officers that Pillgrim was coming down in a Yankee man-of-war?" asked Somers.

"That was his original plan. Though he wrote me from Richmond, I did not know but that he intended to return to the Chatauqua. He gave me no particulars;

did not tell me that his plans had failed, only that he had changed them. When he wrote that he should be on board by the 22d, I knew he was coming down by land, and I corrected my statement. Now, Mr. Somers, will you tell me how you happen to be here?"

"Marine, bring out the other prisoner," said Somers, who had been instructed by Captain Cascabel to confer with the conspirators, if he could obtain any information from them.

The discomfited, crestfallen commander of the Tallapoosa was brought from his room by a marine. He saw Somers, and started back with astonishment. He was pale and haggard, as though he had been spending his time in drinking bad whiskey, and in other debauchery. He had upon his face a fortnight's growth of black beard, and looked more like "Coles" than when Somers had last met him. His captor concluded that his misfortunes on board the Chatauqua had depressed his spirits, in spite of the cool look he had before carried, and that he had given way to dissipation. He certainly appeared like a person who had just come out of a hard "spree."

In the Ben Lomond there was a door opening from the ward-room into the captain's cabin. The vessel had evidently been built for a swift passenger steamer. The ward-room was a portion of the main cabin, from which the steerage and engineers' rooms had been parted off; while the captain's cabin was the original "ladies' saloon." Langdon had been conducted by the marines through this door to the captain's cabin, where the conversation with him had taken place. Pillgrim was in the same manner introduced to this apartment.

"Mr. Somers!" exclaimed the traitor.

"Yes, sir. In the letter you sent me from Old Point Comfort, — and I am greatly obliged to you for the information contained in that letter, — you expressed a hope that you should meet me on board of the Ben Lomond. Your wish has been realized," replied Somers, taking the original letter, with other papers, from his pocket.

Pillgrim trembled in every fibre of his frame. It was not thus he had hoped to meet his enemy.

"'If you capture the Ben Lomond, it will make you a lieutenant. Do it, by all means,'" continued Somers, reading the last paragraph of the letter. "This was your advice. I have done it."

Pillgrim made no reply. His pale, haggard face, darkened by his half-grown beard, was contorted by emotion, and his bloodshot eyes had lost their fire.

"You don't seem to enjoy the situation so much as your letter intimated that you would."

"Mr. Somers. I am your prisoner," said he, with a desperate struggle.

"You are; you will not have the pleasure of hanging me at the yard-arm."

"I am bewildered — overcome."

"So was Langdon."

"I see why you did not join your ship before," said Langdon, with a sneer, as he glanced contemptuously at his principal. "You have been dissipating."

This remark brought forth an angry retort from Pillgrim, and for a few moments each traitor reproached and vilified the other, much to the amusement of the marines, and to the disgust of Somers, who was compelled to interfere. Langdon's severest charge against his late captain was, that he had betrayed their schemes by writing letters, and in other stupid ways. Pillgrim denied it.

"Mr. Somers has just thanked you for the information contained in your letter," sneered Langdon. "He has good reason to do. so."

"I gave him no information that could be of any service to him."

"You gave him the name of the vessel," retorted Langdon.

"But I did not tell him where she was."

"You gave me that information, Mr. Langdon," said Somers, quietly.

"I?"

Somers exhibited the letter in cipher.

"You could not read that without the key," protested the writer of the note.

"The first word I made out was 'Langdon:' the

next, 'Ben Lomond.' I am indebted to both of you. The moral of the whole affair is, that treason cannot prosper. I am indebted to both of you for the information which enabled me to capture the steamer. Gentlemen, it becomes my duty to conduct you on board of the Chatauqua."

"No, Mr. Somers!" groaned Pillgrim, "spare me that."

"I must obey my orders."

The traitor objected strongly to being taken into the presence of the officers of the ship in which he had so recently served. He protested that he had but a few days to live, and begged to be saved from this humiliation. But Somers, though he was not without pity for the degraded and disgraced wretch, had no alternative but to obey the orders of Captain Cascabel.

Langdon accepted his misfortunes with more resignation. He was quite cheerful, and volunteered to tell all he knew, though he was very bitter against Pillgrim, who, he declared, had ruined all their hopes by his dissipation, his silly pretensions, and his reckless exposure of their plans.

Somers was now satisfied that Pillgrim had been intoxicated when he came over the side of the Ben Lomond the night before, which accounted for his violent conduct, and which was one of the accidents which assisted in the easy capture of the vessel.

Both the prisoners were examined on board the Chatauqua; and, with the explanations of Somers, their operations were clearly comprehended. They were placed in confinement, to await the final decision in regard to them. In the forenoon Somers was sent to make his report to the admiral. He was warmly received, judiciously commended, and courteously dismissed. The young officer's respect and admiration for "Brave Old Salt" were not diminished by his second interview.

In the afternoon the Ben Lomond, in charge of an acting ensign, was sent to Pensacola, where she was to remain until further orders. It was surmised that the admiral, not wishing to spare any of the best officers of the fleet, when on the eve of a mighty event, had decided to let the prize remain in port with her prisoners until a more favorable season. Be this as it may, the Old Salamander kept everybody busy for the next ten days, when, the monitors having arrived, and all the ships intended for the attack being in complete readiness, the order was given for the battle, which now stands without a parallel in the annals of naval warfare.

CHAPTER XXV.

THE BATTLE OF MOBILE BAY.

IN order to appreciate the importance of the tremendous action in Mobile Bay, it is necessary to consider that Mobile and Wilmington were the only available ports of the rebels east of the Mississippi. The resources of the Confederacy were exhausted by three years of wasting war, and it was dependent upon foreign supplies for the means of continuing the strife. The earnest attention of the government at Washington, therefore, was directed to the shutting up of these ports.

To form a correct idea of the obstacles to the closing of Mobile Bay, which had been intrusted to Admiral Farragut, it should be remembered that its entrance was guarded by two strongly-built and heavily-armed forts; that the only available channel for large vessels, but three fourths of a mile in width, ran under the guns of Fort Morgan, the stronger of the two forts; that this channel was filled with sunken torpedoes, which, experience had demonstrated, were fatal to any vessels subjected to the explosion; and that the rebels had a fleet of gunboats and iron-clads, which could operate with every advantage against an advancing fleet.

"Brave Old Salt" had estimated all these obstacles, and believing that "success was a duty," he had resolved to overcome them. All the expedients which the ingenuity of a thorough seaman could devise were adopted to strengthen and protect the ships. The plan of the battle was entirely original, and displayed the genius of its author. The admiral modestly declares that he only obeyed the orders of the navy department, and disclaims the credit so lavishly awarded to him by his admiring fellow-citizens; but the government did not tell him how to do it — and in that consisted the doing of it — did not order him to "lash ships" and take his elevated position in the main rigging; did not bid him "butt" the rebel rams with his wooden prows; and for all these things does the whole world sound his praise.

At half past five in the morning the Chatauqua, with the Androscoggin lashed to her port side, took her position in the line of battle. The Brooklyn was to lead the van, with the "Old Hartford," the flag-ship, next in the line, though the doughty old admiral had but tardily acceded to the request of his officers in taking this place. The position of the Chatauqua was in the centre of the line of battle.

At the signal from the admiral, the fleet moved on

Every officer was full of zeal and enthusiasm, though it was certain that some of them would never behold the light of another day; that more or less of the gallant vessels must soon be overwhelmed by the hidden engines of destruction which had been planted in the channel. Somers regarded it as the great day of his existence. He had read his Testament and said his prayers that morning as though it were the last day he had to live, for the most fearful and deadly strife of the whole war was anticipated. A man is never so fully prepared to live well and do his duty faithfully as when he is ready to die.

While the young officer thought even more tenderly than usual of the loved ones in his far-off home, and of that other loved one who was never forgotten when home was remembered, he felt that his country was theirs, and that every blow struck for the nation was struck for them. To die for his country was to die for them — for his own home; and he asked no higher duty than to sacrifice his life, if such was the will of God. "Thy will be done," he repeated many times, though life was full of hopes and joys to him.

The fleet moved on, and the roar of the great guns in the monitors soon announced that the action had commenced. The chase guns of the Chatanqua opened first, and the ship trembled beneath the concussion.

"The Tecumseh has gone down," passed from mouth

to mouth, as a tremendous explosion saluted the ears of the seamen.

The monitor had struck upon a torpedo, and in a moment had disappeared beneath the tide, carrying down with her nearly all her gallant crew. But this incident, appalling as it was even to the battle-scarred veterans on the decks of the fleet, was hardly heeded in the terrible determination of purpose which animated every heart. The Brooklyn paused to dodge some supposed torpedo buoys, and "Brave Old Salt" dashed ahead in the Hartford to his proper place in the van of the battle.

The ships in pairs came up abreast of the fort; and according to the orders of the admiral, the broadside and other guns opened upon the works, not with solid shot, in futile attempts to batter down their dense walls, but with grape, which drove the gunners of the fort from their stations.

Never were guns fired more rapidly; and the roar was tremendous, shaking all earth beneath, and enveloping the scene in dense volumes of smoke, above which, as it occasionally rolled away, might be seen the admiral, lashed to the main rigging of the Hartford. A glimpse at him never failed to call forth the most unbounded enthusiasm, among officers and seamen.

With comparatively little injury the fleet passed the fort, and standing to the north-west to clear the Middle Ground, got out of the reach of its guns. Terrible stories of the torpedoes had been told by deserters and refugees, but the admiral's hopes had been realized; they had been so long in the water that they had become "innocuous."

But a new and greater danger menaced the fleet. The rebel iron-clad Tennessee started out from under the guns of Fort Morgan. She was a formidable adversary; and though the monitors were depended upon to "neutralize" or destroy her, they moved so slowly and steered so badly, that the brunt of the battle was borne by the wooden ships.

"Run her down," was the order from the admiral, which the signal officer interpreted on the quarter deck of the Chatauqua.

Captain Cascabel instantly ordered full head of steam to be put on, and the ship, gathering headway, dashed down upon the Tennessee, striking her at right angles, near the after part of the casemate. The shock of the concussion was terrible. The men were thrown from their feet, and the ship groaned in bitterness of spirit at the hard usage to which she was subjected. Her stem was crushed in to the plank ends, and the water began to pour into the forward store-rooms. Expecting such an event, the carpenter and his gang were at the threatened point, and prevented any disaster from the collision.

The effect upon the iron-clad was hardly perceptible, giving her a heavy list, but apparently inflicting no damage upon her. The Chatauqua swung round as she struck. Captain Cascabel, who had leaped into the mizzen rigging, gave his orders, which were promptly executed by Mr. Hackleford. Solid shot and shell were poured into the ram with a fury which would have been fatal to a less strongly built craft. As it was, one of her port shutters was struck and shattered, the rest of the shot bounding off like peas from an oak floor.

"Hah, you bloody villains of Yankees!" shouted the rebels, at their ports.

"How are you, Johnny Reb?" replied a fore-top man, as he hurled a spittoon in at the port.

Another old salt dashed in a holy-stone, and then the marines opened fire upon them with their muskets.

"Ram her again!" shouted the admiral from the main rigging of the Hartford, as the flag-ship dashed at the game.

The Chatauqua swept round, and succeeded in striking the Tennessee again, but with no better result than before. At the same time she poured in shot and shell from every available gun.

At this moment one of the ships struck the Hartford, by accident, in the dense smoke, and knocked two of her ports into one. It was believed that the flag-ship would go down, for her planking was stove in within two feet of the water-line.

"Save the admiral! save the admiral!" shouted the

men; and there was not one of them who would not have died by fire or water to rescue their beloved leader.

Somers sprang upon the rail, to observe the catastrophe, and to be in readiness to save the admiral if an opportunity occurred. While he stood there, a shot hit the rail diagonally, a splinter struck him in the side, and he dropped helpless into the water.

"Mr. Somers is wounded and fallen overboard!" shouted the captain of the pivot gun amidships.

The words were hardly out of his mouth, before another man dropped into the water from one of the ports. It was Tom Longstone. He found his young friend, and bearing him up with his strong arm, both were rescued from their perilous position.

"She shows the white flag! She surrenders!" was the cry, as the boatswain and Somers reached the deck.

The young officer was borne to the ward-room at the moment of victory, while the cheers of the brave tars were ringing through the fleet.

The Tennessee and the Selma had surrendered, the Gaines had been driven ashore, and the Morgan was for the present safe under the guns of the fort. The victory was complete and decisive.

Somers was severely, if not dangerously, injured. He was borne tenderly to his state-room by his brother officers, as the cheers for the great victory were sounding through the fleet. There had been seven men killed and

The Battle of Mobile Bay. Page 268.

thirty-five wounded on board the Chatauqua. The surgeon was in the cockpit, busily engaged in attending to the wounds of the poor fellows, and could not immediately examine the young officer, who, it was evident, required no surgical operation.

The ship, though considerably cut up by the shots from the fort and from the rebel steamers, was still in condition for active service. The fleet anchored in the bay, out of the reach of the guns of Fort Morgan. Officers were busy in making the necessary surveys, and the men were occupied in repairing damages and restoring order about the decks and rigging.

"How do you feel, Mr. Somers?" asked Mr. Hackleford, entering the sufferer's room, as soon as he could leave the deck.

"I do not suffer much pain, sir; but I am afraid I am badly damaged in the hull," replied Somers, with a languid smile.

He was very pale, and lay very still. He was numb from the effects of the shock given him by the splinter, and some of the functions of his frame seemed to be suspended. The first lieutenant was alarmed, and sent a second messenger for the surgeon, who presently made his appearance, having disposed of the severest cases in the cockpit.

"What do you think of him, doctor?" asked Mr Hackleford.

"I fear he is badly injured," replied Dr. De Plesion, shaking his head.

"Dangerously?" whispered the first lieutenant.

The surgeon shook his head.

"Speak out, doctor," said the patient, faintly. "I am not afraid to die for my country. Please tell me the truth."

"I cannot tell yet, Mr. Somers. Three of the ribs are fractured, but if he is not injured internally, he will do very well," added the surgeon, to Mr. Hackleford.

"I have but little pain," said the patient.

"You will have more, Mr. Somers, by night," continued Dr. De Plesion. "I do not discover any internal injury."

"I hope there is none," said the first lieutenant. "You are too good an officer to be spared, Mr. Somers, — I mean for even a brief period, of course."

The report of the surgeon was anxiously awaited by the captain and all the ward-room officers, for the third lieutenant had been a universal favorite, and his capture of the Ben Lomond, and his gallant conduct during the action with the forts and the Tennessee, had not diminished his popularity. Of all who waited the doctor's decision, none took the matter so much to heart as the boatswain, who had saved him from drowning while he was helpless in the water. Mr. Hackleford noticed him at his duty, still wet to the skin, and kindly gave him permission to visit his young friend.

"I shall not go by the board, Tom," said Somers. "You and I may yet make another cruise together."

"Thank God! I hope so," exclaimed the boatswain, encouraged by these cheerful words.

"Tom, I owe my life to you."

"O, never mind that, my darling! What would I have done if you had slipped your wind?"

"You would have done your duty, as you always do, my good fellow."

"I dare say I should, Mr. Somers, but I can only thank God that you are alive now," replied the boatswain, as the tears flowed down his bronzed cheek, and he turned to leave the room.

CHAPTER XXVI.

IN THE HOSPITAL.

UNDER the arrangement made by Admiral Farragut with the commander of Fort Morgan, the wounded of both sides were sent in the Metacomet to Pensacola. Somers was of the number, and he was borne from his berth in the Chatauqua to the steamer, though the removal caused him great pain. The numbness of his side was beginning to pass away, and the parts to become very sensitive.

"Mr. Somers, I am sorry to see you in this condition," said "Brave Old Salt," who was present with a kind word for the suffering heroes of the battle. "You behaved nobly during the fight, as I am told you always do."

"Thank you, sir. You are very kind," moaned Somers, in his pain and weakness.

"I have not forgotten you, my brave fellow," continued the admiral. "The capture of the Ben Lomond was a matter of more consequence than you can appreciate, perhaps; and your faith and skill in doing this work entitle you to the gratitude of your country."

"I am happy in having merited your approbation."

"You have behaved gallantly in the action; and, I repeat, you shall be remembered. What can I do for you, Mr. Somers?"

"Nothing more for me, admiral. You have done more for me now than I deserve. Mr. Longstone, the boatswain of the Chatauqua, who saved my life —"

"I know all about him, Mr. Somers. He was your right-hand man in the capture of the Ben Lomond."

"He was, sir."

"He shall not be forgotten."

"I have already been rewarded more than I deserve —"

"No, you haven't. Mr. Pillgrim promised you a lieutenant's commission, if you brought out his steamer. I ratify that promise. As to the boatswain, it is a pity he is not an educated man; but he shall be cared for."

"Thank you, sir."

But Somers was too faint to talk any longer, and the admiral passed to other of the noble fellows who had been wounded on that eventful day. The sufferer's cot was placed on the ward-room floor, for the state-rooms and berths were already full. In one of them lay Admiral Buchanan, who had commanded the rebel fleet. He had been wounded in the leg in the battle, and he had lost the battle itself, which, to a proud, brave spirit, was worse than losing a leg.

Somers was now suffering the most intense pain, which he bore like a hero. Tom Longstone bent tenderly over him, his eyes filled with tears, and uttered his adieus. With a hand as gentle as a woman's, he pillowed his head on the couch, and smoothed back his hair from his eyes. He would gladly have gone with his wounded friend, to lave his fevered brow and speak words of comfort and encouragement to him; but neither of them thought of such a thing, for the admiral's fleet was in the enemy's waters, and every man was needed at his post.

The Metacomet, having received her precious freight of mangled heroes, cast off her moorings, and, passing the fort, turned her prow to the eastward. On her arrival at Pensacola, the sufferers were transferred to the hospital, where they received every attention which willing hands and generous hearts could bestow.

Fort Morgan surrendered to the combined forces of the army and navy before the end of the month, and Mobile Bay was in undisputed possession of the government. The work undertaken by the brave admiral had been fully completed. Mobile was now a cipher, so far as the Confederacy was concerned, though a great bluster was made of defending it to the last.

Somers had been three weeks in the hospital, and doubtless owed his life to the skill of the surgeon and the attentions of the nurses. He had been injured internally, as Dr. De Plesion feared; but he had begun to improve, though he was still unable to sit up. He had endured the severest pain, and the doctor had not concealed from him his fears of a fatal result, because the patience and firmness, but especially the religious faith, of the sufferer warranted him in doing so.

Day after day and night after night Somers struggled with his condition, in faith, patience, and resignation. He felt that he was ready to leave the world, full of joys and hopes as it was, for the purer hopes and brighter joys of the eternal world beyond the grave. He thought of his mother, and wished that she might be with him to smooth his dying pillow, if he must die; but it was not the will of God, and he did not murmur. He thought of Kate Portington. He would like to see her once more before he passed away, but this was a vain wish; and from her and the loved ones at home he turned to the glorious realities of the immortal life — fitting theme for one who was trembling between life and death.

In the midst of his pain and earthly loneliness he was happy. He could not but recall the scene of Phil Kennedy's death-bed; of the agony of remorse which shook him, as he looked back upon his past life; of the terrors with which his stricken conscience invested the grave. Then the sufferer, in the deepest depths of his heart, thanked God that he had been enabled to be true to himself and to duty. He was happy in the past, happy in the hope of the future. There was much to regret and to repent of; but as he did regret and repent, he felt that he was forgiven.

He was happy; and the joy of that hour, when an approving conscience triumphs over bodily pain, and decks the waiting tomb with flowers, was worth the struggle with the legions of temptations which all must encounter.

We are best fitted to live when best prepared to die. Somers waited with hope and resignation for the angel of death, but he came not. The very calmness with which he regarded the open tomb, assisted in closing its portals to him. At the end of two weeks the doctor spoke more of life than of death; at the end of three he spoke not at all of the grim messenger — grim he was, even when he wore the chaplet of flowers with which Faith and Hope ever crown him.

Somers was out of danger. The internal inflammation passed away, and the patient began to mend. He thought of life now, of meeting the loved ones who, afar off, had sadly spoken farewells to him when he departed from their presence, with all the fearful perils of storm and battle hanging over him.

On the day after the news of the surrender of Fort Morgan arrived, the Chatauqua dropped her anchor off Pensacola. A boat immediately put off from her, containing Boatswain Longstone, who landed, and hastened to the hospital with all possible speed. Probably there had hardly been an hour since the Metacomet left Mobile Bay with the wounded, in which Tom had not thought of Somers. The old man was as eager and impatient as a child, and could hardly submit to the formalities necessary to procure admission to the hospital.

"My darling!" exclaimed the veteran, as he crept up to the bed of his young friend.

He walked lightly, and spoke softly and tenderly, for he knew how sick Somers had been.

"Ah, Tom, I am glad to see you," replied the patient, as he extended his thin hand, which the boatswain eagerly seized, though he handled it as tenderly as a bashful youth does the hand of the maiden he loves. "It does my eyes good to look upon you, Tom."

"Jack, I've been dying to see you. They told me you were in a bad way, and might slip your cable any moment."

"I have not expected to live, until a week ago."

"God bless you, Jack! I was never so happy in my life;" and the boatswain actually wept, — great, strong, weather-stained veteran as he was, who had breasted the storms of four and thirty years on the ocean.

"I know how you feel, Tom."

"So you may, Jack, — I beg pardon, Mr. — "

"Call me Jack, now," interposed Somers, with a faint smile; "it sounds like old times. You have been the making of me, Tom, and we won't stand on ceremony as long as we are not on board the ship."

The boatswain still held the attenuated hand of his sick friend, and they talked of the past and of the present: of the battle, and of the subsequent events in the bay. But Tom Longstone seemed to be thinking all the time of something else.

"What have you got on, Tom?" asked Somers, as he noticed a "foul anchor" on his shoulder, and a band of gold lace on his sleeve.

"What have I got on? Why, I always wear my colors, of course," replied Tom, with a smile of the deepest satisfaction.

"But those are not the colors of a boatswain in the United States Navy."

"That's a fact, Jack. I'm not a boatswain, just now."

"Indeed!"

"I'm an acting ensign."

"Is it possible?" exclaimed Somers, not less pleased than the veteran.

"It's a fact, my darling; but before we spin any more yarns, here's a document for you. Shall I open it?" continued Tom, as he took from his breast pocket a huge official envelope, whose appearance was entirely familiar to Somers.

"If you please."

It was directed to "Lieutenant John Somers;" and the superscription sufficiently indicated the nature of its contents.

"God bless the admiral!" said Somers.

"God bless the admiral!" repeated Tom, glancing reverently upward as he spoke.

The commission was dated before the news of the battle in Mobile Bay could have reached Washington. It followed the reception of the despatches concerning the capture of the Ben Lomond; and Tom Longstone had been made an acting ensign, though he still retained his warrant as a boatswain, for his conduct in the same affair.

"I congratulate you, Tom, on this promotion," said Somers.

"Thank you, Jack; and I congratulate you as Lieutenant Somers. You are a 'regular,' but I'm only an 'acting,'" replied the veteran. "When the war's over, I shall be a boatswain again."

"I am more rejoiced for you than for myself, Tom."

"Just like you, Jack. If I made you, I'm sure you made me. I got my rating as boatswain's mate in the Rosalie through you, and then I was made a boatswain for what I did with you. Now I'm an ensign by your doings. I suppose you think I'm not up to it, Jack."

"Yes, I do. I know you are. There's nothing about a ship that you don't know as well as the admiral himself, except —"

"Except," laughed Tom, as Somers paused, "except what?"

"Navigation."

"I know something about that, Jack — I do, upon my honor."

"I do not doubt it."

"When I first went into the navy, I was a regular sea dandy. I used big words, as long as the coach-whip; but I soon found a man must not talk above his station. When I was a young man, I wasn't a bad scholar. I went to the academy, and learned surveying; I meant to be a surveyor; but I got a hitch, and went to sea."

"A hitch?"

"Well, I never mention it now. Squire Kent's daughter didn't treat me as handsomely as she did another young fellow, and I drank more liquor than was good for me. I got run down; and when I had payed out all the respectability I had, I went to sea. That cured me of drinking; in fact, I became a temperance man before the grog rations were stopped in the navy. As I said, I was pretty well educated, and talked as well as the officers on the quarter deck. But my shipmates laughed at me, and I soon dropped down into using sea slang."

"I have noticed that your speech has been wonderfully improved since you were made a boatswain."

"I've been trying to cure my bad habits. I've been lying round loose in the navy for thirty years before the war began. I tried to be honest and true, but the war has set me right up. I haven't told you the best of the news yet, Jack."

"What more?"

"You are appointed to the Ben Lomond as prize master, and I'm going with you as second officer. The admiral says you shall take the prize home, if she has to wait two months for you. She is yours, and you shall have the command of her."

"He is very kind; but I do not think I shall be able to take command at present."

"We are to go as soon as the doctor will let you be carried on board of her. Jack, the Ben Lomond is going into the navy; and if I mistake not, she will be in command of Lieutenant Somers."

"That would be the height of my ambition. Indeed, I never aspired to anything so great as the command of a fine steamer."

"You'll have her; the admiral is your friend. If you do, I shall be in the ward-room. Splinter my timber-heads! Only think of that! Tom Longstone a ward-room officer!"

"You deserve it, Tom."

In the course of the week, other officers of the Chatauqua visited the patient, and at the end of that period the doctor permitted Somers to be conveyed on board the Ben Lomond.

CHAPTER XXVII.

MISS PORTINGTON NOT AT HOME.

PILLGRIM and Langdon had been in close confinement at Pensacola since their capture. They were now placed on board of the Ben Lomond to be sent north. An apartment was specially fitted up for their use in the steerage, for they were regarded as dangerous men, to whom bolts, bars, and other obstacles, were but trifling impediments. A sufficient number of marines to guard them were detailed for duty on the passage, and the steamer sailed for Boston, where the prize was to be adjusted.

Somers was now improving very rapidly, and before he left the hospital, had sat up a small portion of each day. The pleasant intelligence brought to him by Tom Longstone had not retarded his recovery; on the contrary, the bright hopes of the future which it suggested, rather stimulated his feeble frame, and assisted in his restoration to health.

The steamer had fine weather on the passage, with the exception of a gale of thirty hours' duration. She put into Hampton Roads, and landed her prisoners at Fortress Monroe, in accordance with the orders of her commander, and then proceeded to Boston. The Ben Lomond behaved remarkably well in the heavy weather she experienced, proving herself to be a strongly-built and substantial vessel. Somers sent his despatches to Washington from Fortress Monroe.

When the Ben Lomond sailed into Boston Harbor, Somers was able to go on deck, for with each day of the voyage his health had continued to improve. The steamer was duly handed over to the naval authorities, and the young lieutenant was granted a furlough of sixty days.

"Our cruise is up," said Tom Longstone, when the business had been completed.

"For the present, we have nothing to do; but I hope we shall soon receive our orders," replied Somers. "Now, Tom, you will go down to Pinchbrook with me, and spend a couple of months."

"Thank you, Jack; I hardly think I should know how to behave in a house on shore, it is so long since I have been in one."

"You will soon learn."

They went to Pinchbrook, and Tom received a welcome almost as cordial as that extended to Somers. The veteran was soon made entirely at home by his young friend's father, and such a "spinning of yarns" for thirty days had never been known before. Tom told a story of the Cumberland; then Captain Somers had a West India yarn; and gran'ther Greene was indulgently permitted to relate his experience in the "last war," though it was observed that the old man, whose memory was much impaired, always told the same story.

Never did a happier trio gather around a kitchen fire than that which sat around the cook-stove at Pinchbrook on those autumn mornings. Very likely Mrs. Somers thought the "men folks" were in the way at times; but she was too much interested in the stories told, and too good natured to raise an objection, especially when John joined the party.

In the mean time, Somers was rapidly regaining his health and strength. As may be supposed, he was a lion in Pinchbrook, and was invited to every party and every merry-making in the place. Captain Barney was with him a great deal, and was as fond of him as though he had been his own son. Of course the young ladies of Pinchbrook regarded the lieutenant as a great man; and if it had not been known in town that he was "paying attention" to a commodore's daughter, he might have been absolutely persecuted by the fair ones of his native village.

In strict observance of his promise, Somers had written several letters to Kate Portington, but had received no answer. These epistles, with the exception of an occasional playful remark, were confined to the details of his naval operations. The events of his career were faithfully recorded, and they were in no sense such productions as many silly young men would have written under similar circumstances. No answer to any of them had been received.

Since his arrival at Pinchbrook, Somers had written two letters; but at the end of the first month of his furlough, he had not heard a word from Kate. He was troubled, and no doubt thought Kate was very cold and cruel. He knew that Pillgrim had not seen her, and therefore could not have prejudiced her against him. It was possible that his letters had not reached their destination; Kate might be away from home; and he was not willing to believe that anything had occurred to make her less friendly to him than formerly.

Somers, as we have so often had occasion to represent him, was always in favor of "facing the music." If there was anything the matter, he wanted to know it. If the lady wished to discontinue the acquaintance, he wanted to know that; and when he could no longer content himself in Pinchbrook, with the question unsettled, he started for Newport. On his arrival he proceeded at once to the residence of Commodore Portington. With a firm hand he rang the bell — in surprising contrast with his first visit, for now he was firm and decided.

The servant informed him that Miss Portington was at

home, and he sent up his card. Somers sat nervously waiting the issue. Presently the servant returned and handed him a card, on which was written, "*Miss Portington is not at home to Mr. John Somers.*"

He was confounded by this cool reply. Though her present conduct was in accordance with the unanswered letters, he had not expected to be thus rudely repelled. If she had any objection to him, why didn't she tell him so? He had done his duty to his country, and kept his promises to her. It was the severest blow he had ever received.

He read the card, rose from his chair, and left the house, as dignified as though he had been on the quarter deck of the Ben Lomond. He was too proud to ask or to offer any explanations. We will not undertake to say how bad he felt. Perhaps he wished he had died in the Pensacola hospital, when he lay at death's door; perhaps he felt like rushing into the hottest of a fight, and laying down his life for the cause he had espoused, without thinking that this would be suicide, rather than a generous sacrifice to a holy duty.

Mr. Pillgrim had informed him that he would meet with a "chilly" reception. It was even worse than that; but as it was evidently caused by the traitor's machinations, he was content to suffer. If she chose to let the words of the wretched conspirator against his country bias her against him, he could not help it; and his only remaining duty was to submit with the best possible grace.

Of course he could not leave Newport without calling at the Naval Academy. Mr. Revere, the commandant of midshipmen, was his firm friend, and it would be treason to him to leave the city without seeing him. He was cordially received, and his experience in Mobile Bay was listened to with the most friendly interest.

"I need not ask you if you have been to Commodore Portington's," said Mr. Revere.

"I have, sir."

"Well, how is Miss Portington?"

"I did not see her," replied Somers, who, conscious that he had done no wrong, was not disposed to conceal his misfortune from so good a friend.

"Did not see her!" exclaimed the commandant.

Somers explained.

The story of Pillgrim's treason had been circulated, but the particulars by which it had been exposed were known to only a few. Mr. Revere saw at once the cause of the rupture.

"The villain has sent her the bond you signed," said he.

"Perhaps he has."

"Probably she knows nothing of the circumstances under which you signed it."

"I have had no opportunity to explain."

"But, Somers, you musn't be too stiff. Any lady would be fully justified in refusing to see a gentleman who signed a paper like that, which contained her name in such a connection."

"I think so myself; and therefore I will not blame her."

"Pillgrim got you to sign that document for this very purpose."

"I surmised as much."

"But it is a wrong to the lady as well as to you, to permit this thing to go on."

"I have no remedy."

"Write her a note, explaining your position."

"My motives would be misconstrued."

"Then I shall act for you."

Somers went to his hotel, and Mr. Revere did act it for him. Kate was not satisfied. A high-minded man would have died rather than sign such a paper. So would Somers, if the bond had any real meaning. The commandant was not successful in the negotiation, as mediators seldom are in such cases.

"I am satisfied, Mr. Revere," said Somers: but he was as far from satisfied as a young man could be.

"There is no help for it; but, Somers, I have invited a few friends to my house this evening, and you must be with us."

"Will Miss Portington be there?"

"She has been invited, with her mother."

"I will go," replied he, still carrying out his principle that it is always best to " face the music."

He did go. The few friends were about fifty — to celebrate the birthday of the commandant's lady. There were music, and dancing, and revelry; and Kate Portington was there, with her mother. He saw the fair girl; saw her smile as pleasantly and unconcernedly as though nothing had happened. He met her face to face; she bowed coldly, and passed on. Mrs. Portington was not quite so "chilly," but not at all as she had been in former times.

"Mr. Somers, we shall always remember you with gratitude, for the service you so kindly rendered us," said she.

"It is hardly worth remembering, madam, much less mentioning," replied Somers.

"It shall always be gratefully remembered, and cordially mentioned. You cannot yourself regret more than I do, that anything should have occurred to disturb the pleasant relations which formerly existed."

"I regret it very much, madam; but as I think I have done my duty to my country and to my friends, I must regret it without reproaching myself for my conduct in that which has proved so offensive."

"Was it your duty to sign that vile paper?" asked the lady, in excited tones.

"I think it was."

"I must take a different view of the matter; but, Mr. Somers, I shall still be interested in your success."

"Thank you, madam."

And the lady passed on. Somers looked at Kate. She was dancing with a young officer who had greatly distinguished himself in the waters of North Carolina. She looked happy. Was she so? She certainly had a wonderful command of herself if she was not. Somers retired at an early hour.

Did Kate think he was an adventurer? His superior officer had directed him to sign the bond, as a "war measure." He had done so with regret and disgust. The paper meant nothing to him. Why should it mean anything to her and her mother?

The next day, Somers returned to Pinchbrook, where he found certain official documents in the post office, directed to him. He was appointed to the command of the Firefly, which was the new name given by the department to the Ben Lomond. The steamer had been duly condemned, and purchased by the government, her great speed admirably adapting her as a cruiser for rebel pirates. Somers was generously rewarded for his zeal and success in the capture of the twin steamers, which had been intended to prey on the commerce of the country.

Acting Ensign Longstone was appointed second lieutenant of the Firefly. The third and fourth lieutenants, and the sailing master, were acting ensigns, like Tom Longstone.

All was excitement now at the cottage in Pinchbrook, in anticipation of Somers's departure. A lieutenant commanding was a higher position than he had ever hoped to obtain; but even while he rejoiced over his bright future, he could not help being "blue" over his affair at Newport. He tried to forget the fair lady, but he found that was not an easy matter. He devoted himself to the fitting up of the Firefly, spending part of his time at Pinchbrook, till his orders came from Washington. A kind word from Kate would have made him the happiest man in the world. As that did not come, he went to sea without it.

CHAPTER XXVIII.

THE BEN LEDI.

THE Firefly had been strengthened and otherwise improved for the purpose to which she was to be applied. Her armament had been changed, to adapt it to the standard of the United States navy. She now carried a hundred pounder rifle amidships, a rifled thirty on her forecastle, four twenty-four pounders on the broadsides, and two howitzers on the quarter deck. The cabin, ward-room, and steerage remained as before.

It was a pleasant November day — in the full reign of the Indian summer — when she went down the harbor. Somers stood on the quarter deck, as dignified as the commander of a man-of-war should be, but he could hardly repress the feeling of pride and exultation with which he regarded his position. He was hardly twenty-one, though he was mature enough in appearance and in judgment for twenty-five. He had realized the warmest hope he had permitted himself to cherish. He was in command of a beautiful vessel, with a hundred officers and men under his charge. He was the supreme authority; every man on board touched his cap to him.

Below was a cabin, appropriated wholly to his use, where he could live as luxuriously as a lord. He had no watch to keep, no work to perform. As he contemplated his position, he was absolutely amazed. He had hoped, but not expected, to reach this pinnacle of his ambition. But there was another side to the question. A fearful responsibility was imposed upon him. The lives of his hundred men depended upon him. This valuable steamer, with her armament and stores, was intrusted to him, and he must account for all loss or waste on board of her. More than this, the honor of the flag under which he sailed had been committed to him. If he lost his ship by bad management, it would be his ruin. If he permitted the ensign which floated at his peak to be disgraced, it would be infamy to him.

In the public service he might have occasion to run into foreign ports, or to visit neutral waters. His want of knowledge, or his want of judgment, might entangle his country in perplexing broils with other nations, or even involve her in another war. As he thought of his delicate and difficult duties, he felt like shrinking from them, and avoiding the immense responsibility. Being "captain," in this view, was quite a different thing from what he had anticipated.

With a smile he recalled his own reflections, when, as

an ordinary seaman, he had observed the captain of his ship walk the deck. Then he had thought the commander had the easiest and jolliest time of all the men on board, with his fine cabin all to himself, and no watch to keep, and apparently no work to do. From his present stand-point, the captain occupied the most difficult and trying place in the ship, and he almost wished he had declined the command offered to him.

Outside the bay, the sealed orders were opened. As he had anticipated, he was ordered to cruise in search of rebel steamers, whose depredations on the coast had severely tried the patience of the nation. He was directed to proceed first to the eastward, and then to use his own judgment. There were several rebel privateers, or naval vessels belonging to the Confederacy. The Tallahassee, the Chickamauga, and the Olustee had been the most mischievous; and it was believed that there were others at Wilmington, and the *neutral* ports of New Brunswick, Nova Scotia, and the West Indies.

Having learned where he was to go, and what he was to do, he went on deck and gave his orders to Mr. Gamage, the first lieutenant. The Firefly was headed to the north-east, and all sail set to help her along. Before Somers went below, she logged fifteen knots, which was splendid for a ship with her bunkers full of coal.

In the evening the young commander invited Tom Longstone to visit his cabin. The veteran was in his happiest frame of mind. All the aspirations of his earlier years seemed to have been rekindled in his soul; he had abandoned the use of slang, and conducted himself so much like a gentleman, outwardly, that no one could have suspected he had spent thirty odd years of his life before the mast; but as he had always been a gentleman at heart, it was comparatively easy for him to assume the externals of his new profession.

The old man had donned a new uniform; and though his hair and beard were iron gray, he looked as "spruce" as a dry goods clerk. No change of dress, however, could make him any other than an "old salt." He walked with a rolling gait, and had all the airs of a veteran seaman. It is true that in the transposition from the forecastle to the ward-room he had discarded "pigtail," and confined himself to "fine cut," taken from a silver box; but he still used as much of the "weed" as an old sheet-anchor man.

"You sent for me, Captain Somers," said the second lieutenant, as he touched his foretop, from the force of habit.

"Sit down, Mr. Longstone," said the captain. "It is one of the blessings of my present position that I have a place to sit down and talk with old friends. I suppose you know we are bound to the eastward in search of rebel privateers."

"So Mr. Gamage told me, sir. I hope we shall catch some of them."

"So do I; but I'm afraid we are on a wild-goose chase."

"Perhaps not — at least, I hope not. If there is a rebel ship in these waters, we'll have her, if we have to dive after her."

"The ocean is very broad. None of our ships have had much luck in catching these rebel pirates. I would rather have gone down on the blockade, where there is some show for us."

"Don't give it up, Captain Somers."

"I don't give it up; but I do not see any reason why I should be more fortunate than others. A score of our ships have cruised for months without catching a single one of them."

"They didn't look where they were," laughed Tom.

"If I knew where they were, I would look there."

"You will certainly catch one of the pirates, Captain Somers."

"Why do you say so?"

"Because you are smart, and you are lucky. I know you will make a capture on this cruise. I feel it in my bones."

"I hope I shall. Wouldn't it be glorious, if I could send such a despatch as Captain Winslow did, after he had sunk the Alabama?"

Somers's eyes glistened as he thought of it, but it was only an air-castle; and after he had contemplated it for a moment, his common sense obliged him to come down from the clouds.

The cruise of the Firefly would supply matter enough for a whole volume, but we have only space for a mere outline of the voyage. The steamer lay off and on for a week without meeting with anything that looked like a rebel privateer, when her commander decided to run into Halifax, where he hoped to obtain some information. The city was a nest of "secesh sympathizers," and the captain of the Firefly was not received with much enthusiasm outside of the American consulate. He had not been in the habit of hearing his country and her rulers vilified, and as he sat in the parlor of the hotel, and listened to hostile remarks, evidently intended for his ear, nothing but prudence prevented him from indulging in the luxury of pulling the noses of the speakers. He preserved his dignity in spite of his inclination.

"Upon my word, this is a very unexpected pleasure," said a familiar voice.

He looked up from the newspaper he was reading. Before him stood Mr. Pillgrim!

"Quite as unexpected to me as to you, Mr. Pillgrim!" replied Somers, with abundant self-possession.

"I dare say, Mr. Somers," laughed Pillgrim. "Of course you did not expect to see me. Will you take a glass of wine with me, Mr. Somers?"

"No, I thank you; I never indulge — as you are aware."

"I didn't know but your rapid advancement had changed your tastes."

"No, sir."

"You command the Ben Lomond now, Mr. Somers, I learn from the papers."

"The Firefly is her present name."

"Bah! What an ugly name for a fine steamer like her. The Tallapoosa is much better. Be that as it may, I congratulate you on your promotion and your appointment; and you know how sincere I am!"

"I do know; and, therefore, cannot even thank you for your good wishes."

"Don't be savage, Mr. Somers. You can afford to be very good-natured."

"I am."

"You don't seem to be very glad to see me."

"On the contrary, I am. I hope, with your usual candor, that you will tell me what you are going to do next, and give me an opportunity to cut out your vessel. I am up here for that purpose."

Pillgrim bit his lip.

"At present, Mr. Somers, I must be silent; but we shall yet meet and settle up old accounts. Let us not be ill-natured. If we meet as enemies, we will fight it out."

"We can never meet in any other way."

"That isn't friendly. How is Miss Portington?"

"She was well, last time I saw her;" and Somers blushed, and looked disconcerted — as he really was,

"I am glad to hear it, Mr. Somers," said Pillgrim, significantly.

Somers changed the topic at once, and finally contrived to ask the traitor how he happened to be in Halifax, instead of Fortress Monroe. Pillgrim laughed exultingly, and declared there were no irons, bolts, or bars that could keep him a prisoner; and the facts seemed to justify the assertion.

"Mr. Somers, not more than one half of the people of the North are in favor of this cruel war. I have friends in Washington and other cities whom no one suspects of favoring the South. I am indebted to them for my liberation. I shall yet carry out my original purpose. I have lost three vessels. I was paid for two by the Confederacy; and I have your bond for half the value of the third. I am a commander in the Confederate navy. In one week I shall be at sea. I shall sink, burn, and destroy! You can't help yourself."

"Is your ship here?"

"Yes — no."

Pillgrim laughed, turned on his heel, and walked away. Somers was excited. He wanted to know more. He went to the American consul. A "blue-nose" sailor of the Firefly was sent on shore, who found Pillgrim, and without much difficulty shipped in the "Sunny South" for a voyage on the coast. This was all the information that could be obtained. There was no such

26

craft as the Sunny South in port. Somers examined all the vessels in the harbor, and found a steamer called the Ben Ledi — another Scottish mountain. She was Clyde-built, and similar to the Ben Nevis and the Ben Lomond. The name alone satisfied the inquirer that she belonged to the same family as the two vessels he had already captured.

Things began to look a little more hopeful, and the young commander carefully read his books on international law. He attempted to place the Firefly where he could watch the suspected steamer; but the authorities, on various pretences, prevented him from doing so. The next morning the Ben Ledi was gone. Somers was exceedingly mortified, for he might as well look for a needle in a haymow as try to find the vessel on the ocean. He put to sea at once. A "blue-nose" official laughed at him as his gig pulled off to the ship, and everybody on shore was in high glee because the Confederate had eluded the Yankee.

Somers kept cool in spite of his chagrin; and believing the Ben Ledi would run for Wilmington, where she would probably be fitted out as a cruiser, he headed the Firefly in that direction, and gave chase.

CHAPTER XXIX.

A LONG CHASE.

SOMERS was somewhat bewildered by the events which had transpired during his brief stay at Halifax. It was almost incredible that Pillgrim had again escaped; but the traitor had powerful friends — men who appeared to be loyal while they were in full sympathy with the leaders of the rebellion. The three "Bens," the last of which was now fleeing before him, were certainly an interesting family. Pillgrim, while abroad, and operating for the Southern Confederacy, had apparently purchased a whole line of Clyde-built steamers. Two of them were now in good hands, and doing good service to the loyal cause; but Somers feared that the third would escape him.

Pillgrim had learned prudence from the experience of the past. Somers hoped he would indulge in his customary reckless boasting; that his thirst for revenge would again lead him to betray himself; but he had not dropped even a hint that could be of any service. The decoy seaman had only learned that he was to sail in the

"Sunny South." The sudden departure of the Ben Ledi was the only important fact in possession of the commander of the Firefly.

When the ship was well out of the bay, and her course laid down, Somers went into his cabin to consult his charts, and consider a plan for future operations. Unfortunately there was no information on which to base a theory in regard to the pirate's course. He could only guess at her destination. The Firefly was run at her best speed during the rest of the day, but her course for a large portion of the time was through a dense Nova Scotia fog, and nothing was seen or heard.

On the following day, the sun shone through a clear air, and at noon there was seen, dead ahead, some evidences of black smoke in the horizon. This was a hopeful sign, for there was a steamer burning English coal in the direction indicated. It might be the Ben Ledi, and it might not; but the appearance created a tremendous excitement on board the Firefly.

"Captain Somers, you will have her," said Tom Longstone, placing himself by the side of the young commander. "It is your luck."

"That may not be the steamer we are after. We haven't seen her yet."

"That's the Ben Ledi; you may depend upon it. I wouldn't give five cents to any man to guarantee my share of prize money in her."

" Don't be too confident, Mr. Longstone."

" She is ours, Captain Somers."

" I wish I could believe it."

" You must believe it, and work for it."

" I shall certainly work for it."

And he did work for it. Everything that would add a fraction of a knot to the speed of the Firefly was done. The black smoke was visible all the rest of the day, but not a sight of the steamer from which it proceeded could be obtained. Darkness settled down upon the ocean, and nothing could be seen during the night. The next day was cloudy, and there was not a sign of encouragement to those on board of the pursuing vessel. Then came a gale of twenty hours' duration; but the Firefly held her course, and proved herself to be a perfect sea boat.

The fourth day out from Halifax was fine, and shortly after sunrise the cloud of black smoke was again discovered, and a thrill of delight coursed through the veins of Somers as he discovered it. The steamer was on the port bow now, but it was evident that both steamers were bound to the same point, though their courses had slightly varied during the gale.

" I told you so, Captain Somers!" exclaimed Lieutenant Longstone, as he rubbed his hands briskly in view of the bright prospect.

" We haven't caught her yet, Mr. Longstone."

"But you will catch her, just as sure as the sun shines."

"Mr. Pillgrim will not allow himself to be taken."

"He cannot help himself."

"Perhaps he can. That steamer sails as well as the Firefly, and we are not a hundred and fifty miles from Cape Fear."

"No matter; we have got ten hours' working time, and we shall use her up. Shall we put the helm to starboard, Captain Somers?"

"No; keep her as she is," replied the commander. "If she is going into Wilmington we shall be making something on this tack. We have the weather-gage of her."

It was soon clearly demonstrated that the chase had "slowed down," so as not to approach the coast before night should favor her operations, though her great speed gave her every advantage over an ordinary pursuer. The Firefly had run down so that the Ben Ledi was on her port beam, about eight miles distant. Both steamers had hoisted English colors, for Somers had no idea of being cheated out of the game by "showing his hand."

The most intense excitement prevailed on board of the Firefly, for it was evident that a few hours more would settle the question one way or the other. Somers was not disposed to wait until night, which would favor the chase more than himself; and he was afraid, if he headed towards her, that she would take the alarm and beat him on time. He kept quiet for a couple of hours, just as though he were waiting for the darkness to cover him in running the blockade.

His plan seemed to be a success, for after a while the Ben Ledi began to bear down upon him. It was an anxious hour for Somers. He ordered the first lieutenant to beat to quarters, and the chief engineer to have on a full head of steam. The guns were loaded with solid shot, and every preparation made for an exciting time. Pillgrim did not seem to suspect thus far that the steamer under English colors was the one he had left in Halifax harbor. It was certain that he did not yet recognize her.

The Firefly reciprocated the attention of the Ben Ledi, and moved slowly towards her, for Somers was careful not to excite suspicion by being precipitate. The two steamers approached within three miles, and the respective captains were busy in examining each other's ship through their glasses. The chase now hoisted her number. As Somers had the Lloyd's signal book, he read it without difficulty. It was the Ben Ledi. To the question, "What ship is that?" he had no answer to give, for it was not prudent to hoist the old number of the Ben Lomond.

Our younger readers may not understand how a conversation is carried on between ships at sea, several miles distant from each other. There are ten small signal flags representing the nine digits and the **zero.** Any number can of course be formed of these figures. **Every ship is provided** with **a number,** which if it consists of two figures is represented **by** two flags, hoisted together; **three** figures, three flags; and **so on.**

The signal book also contains a great **number of questions** and answers, such **as,** "What ship is that?" "Where bound?" "**All well.**" "Short of water," &c. Each sentence has its **invariable** number, which may be indicated by the signal flags. If one vessel shows **the** number 124, the captain of the ship signalized would find this number in his signal **book**; and against **it would be printed the question** or answer.

Somers **was** not disposed **to reply** to the question of Pillgrim; **and as he** did not do so, the traitor immediately took the **alarm.** The Ben Ledi went about, and made off to the eastward under full steam. The Firefly was all ready to follow, and then commenced **a** most exciting chase. It was useless to waste shot at that distance, and **Somers** confined his attention to the speed of his vessel. For three hours the pursuit was continued, without any perceptible decrease of the distance between the two steamers.

But it was soon discovered that Pillgrim was gradually **wearing round. Somers** perceived his intention, but it was not prudent to attempt to cut him off all at once, by taking the arc of a smaller circle; but he worked his ship slowly round; and when both vessels were headed to the west, he had gained a mile. Pillgrim had evidently made up his mind to go into Wilmington at any risk, though under ordinary circumstances the more prudent course would have been for him to continue at sea, where a dark night or a fog might have enabled him to elude his pursuer. Somers concluded, therefore, that the Ben Ledi was short of coal, for his own supply was nearly exhausted.

The furnaces of the Firefly were now worked to their utmost capacity, and every expedient to make steam was resorted to by the excited engineers and firemen. There was a stiff breeze from the south-west, and both vessels had crowded on every stitch of canvas that could be spread. It had already been demonstrated that there was no appreciable difference in the speed of the two steamers, and the result of the chase was to depend entirely upon the management of each.

When the two vessels had come about so as to make a fair wind, the Firefly had been the first to spread her canvas, and the superior discipline of her crew was thus made apparent. A slight advantage had thus been gained, and it was certain that "the balance of power" lay in the sails. At meridian an observation was obtained, and the position of the ship was accurately laid down on the chart. The latitude was 33° 59′ 7″; the longitude 76° 29′ 23″. To make the Swash Channel, which was covered by the guns of Fort Fisher, the Ben Ledi would have laid a course about half a point south of west; but her present course was west-south-west. Somers, after examining his chart, had some doubts whether she was going into Wilmington.

Tom Longstone had the deck during the afternoon watch. He was a veteran seaman, and his experience had made him more familiar with canvas than with steam. With the most anxious solicitude he watched the sails during the afternoon, and under his skilful directions they were kept perfectly trimmed. On that momentous occasion everything was reduced down to the finest point, as well in the handling of the engine as the tacks, sheets, and halliards.

The case was hopeful, though the gain could not be perceived in one, or two, hours; but at eight bells hardly a mile lay between the contending steamers. The first lieutenant wanted to open on the chase with the rifled gun on the top-gallant forecastle; but Somers refused permission, for while he was gaining on the Ben Ledi only in inches, he could not afford to lose feet by the recoil of the gun, until there was a better chance of hitting the mark. At two bells in the first dog watch, just as the sun was setting, the Ben Ledi doubled Frying Pan Shoals, passing close to the breakers. Then, as her people discovered a couple of vessels belonging to the blockading squadron, she sheered off, and went to the westward.

These changes, with the doubt and uncertainty which prevailed on board of the Ben Ledi, had been very favorable to the Firefly, now within half a mile of her. Two vessels from the blockading fleet had started to engage in the exciting work, but they were too late to help or hinder the pursuit. Somers gave the order to fire upon the Ben Ledi, which was now endeavoring to work round to the Beach Channel.

Though the darkness had settled down upon the chase, the Firefly continued the pursuit with unabated vigor. Her pilot was familiar with the channels, bars, and shoals. Shot after shot was fired at the Ben Ledi, and it was soon evident that one of them had in some way damaged her wheels, for she was rapidly losing ground. But now a battery on Oak Island suddenly opened on the Firefly.

"We must end this thing," said Somers, as a shot from the fort whizzed over his head.

"Yes, sir," replied the first lieutenant. "We can hardly pass that battery."

"Try the hundred pounder."

When the pivot gun was ready, the Firefly swung round, and the heavy piece roared out its salutation to the blockade runner. It was aimed by Tom Longstone, and the bolt struck the Ben Ledi square in the stern, breaking in her counter, and leaving her helpless on the water. The Firefly stopped her wheels. A shot from the fort crushed through her smoke-stack.

The chase, completely disabled, drifted on the beach and grounded, under the guns of the battery. The Firefly now poured shell into her from every gun that could be brought to bear. In a few moments a sheet of flame rose from her, and lighted up the channel for miles around, clearly revealing to the gunners in the fort the exact position of Somers's vessel.

The work had been accomplished, the Ben Ledi had been destroyed, and the Firefly hastened to escape from her dangerous locality. In coming about she poured a parting broadside into the burning steamer. As she swung round, a hail from the water was heard, and a boat containing several men was discovered. It had been carried by the tide away from the beach. The occupants were taken on board, though one of them was wounded and utterly helpless. They had no oars, and were in danger of being carried out to sea.

"Here's the cap'n: he was hit by a piece of a shell," said one of the men.

"Who is he?" asked Somers.

"Cap'n Pillgrim."

The sufferer was taken down into the ward-room, and the surgeon began to examine him as the Firefly steamed down the channel under a shower of shot and shell from the battery.

"How is he?" asked the young commander, when the ship had passed out of the reach of the guns of the fort.

"He is dead!" replied the surgeon.

"Dead! Good Heaven!" exclaimed Somers, impressed by the terrible retribution which had at last overtaken the traitor.

"Yes, sir; he died a few moments since. A fragment of a shell tore open his breast and penetrated his lungs," added the surgeon.

"That's the last of him," said Lieutenant Longstone. "He will lay no more plots."

"He has been a dangerous enemy to his country," continued Somers. "If he had succeeded in running in with that vessel, he would have obtained her armament, and made terrible havoc among the merchant ships on the coast. He was a daring fellow; he was reckless at times. He told me on board of the Chatauqua that he had purchased three steamers in Scotland; this is the last one."

"Three Bens," added Tom. "Captain Somers, you have had a hand in capturing and destroying them all."

"I have; and it is really marvellous, when I think of it."

"I knew you would capture the Ben Ledi," continued the second lieutenant, exultingly.

"I did not capture her."

"It is the same thing."

"You will not find it so when your prize money is distributed."

"A fig for the prize money," replied Tom, contemptuously. "We destroyed her; and it's all the same thing. I would rather have had that villain hanged than killed by an honest shell; but there is no help for it now."

"Peace, Mr. Longstone; he is dead now. We have nothing more to do with him."

The body of Mr. Pillgrim was laid out in a proper place, and as the coal bunkers of the Firefly were nearly empty, she was headed for Port Royal, where she arrived on the afternoon of the following day. On the passage, the men from the Ben Ledi, who had been picked up in the boat, were examined in regard to their knowledge of her ultimate use. One of the party was an intelligent English seaman, who acknowledged that he had shipped, for the Confederate navy, in the Sunny South, which was to be the new name of the Ben Ledi. She had waited a month at Halifax for orders. Langdon was not on board of her, and the seaman had no knowledge of any such person.

The Firefly had not been seen on board the Sunny South until both steamers were off Wilmington. After passing Frying Pan Shoals, a shot from the Firefly had partially crippled her port wheel, which accident had caused her to lose ground rapidly. The projectile from the hundred pounder had completely shattered her stern, and disabled her rudder, and knocked the engine " all in a heap." The port quarter boat was torn to pieces by a shell, the same which had given Pillgrim his mortal wound. The after tackle of the other quarter boat had been shot away, and when it was dropped into the water the oars were gone. Most of the crew had saved themselves by swimming ashore. The Ben Ledi had a valuable cargo, which the informer declared was totally destroyed by fire or water.

On her arrival at Port Royal, the Firefly coaled without delay; the body of Pillgrim was buried, and after forwarding his despatches to the navy department by a supply steamer, Somers sailed again on another cruise after privateers, Confederate cruisers, and blockade runners. The Tallahassee and the Chickamauga were supposed to be at Wilmington, but the Olustee was believed to be still afloat. Of this cruise our limits do not permit us to record details; but the Firefly captured a valuable steamer in December, and sent her into port. This was the only prize she obtained; and being short of coal, she ran into Boston, on New Year's day, where her prize had arrived before her.

Somers immediately forwarded his despatches, and awaited the orders of the department. Of course he hastened down to Pinchbrook as soon as he could leave the ship, where he was heartily welcomed and warmly congratulated upon his successful cruise.

"Here's something for you, John," said Mrs. Somers, taking a daintily made up letter from the mantel-piece, when the welcome had been given, kisses bestowed, and hands shaken. "It has been here a fortnight."

Somers knew the handwriting, for it had often gladdened his heart before, and a flush came to his cheeks as he tore open the envelope. It was from Kate Portington, whom the young commander had not failed to think of every day during his absence, though it was with pain and sorrow at the rupture which had separated them. The letter healed his only wound.

"I shall never forgive myself," she wrote, "for my harsh treatment of you; and I am afraid you can never forgive me. I have seen Mr. Hackleford, who says that he ordered you to sign that horrible paper. Why didn't you tell me so, John?" He would have told her so, if she had given him an opportunity. But she was repentant, and Somers was rejoiced.

The letter was four pages in length, and among all the pleasant things it contained, the pleasantest was that she was spending a month in Boston, at the residence of a friend, where she hoped to see him.

She did see him there, on the very day he received the letter. What passed between them we are not at liberty to say in a book of this kind, except to inform the reader that Kate was herself again; that in the joy of meeting him after this painful rupture, she actually forgot to be proper, and in spite of her promise, and her mother's lecture, she called him "prodigy." The past, the present, and the future, were discussed, and Somers went on board the Firefly the happiest of mortals.

27*

CHAPTER XXX.

THE END OF THE REBELLION.

THE Firefly, with her energetic young commander, was too serviceable to be permitted long to remain in idleness, and she was ordered to join Admiral Porter's squadron, which had failed to capture Fort Fisher in December; or rather, the military portion of the expedition had failed to do it, for the navy had done its part of the work to the satisfaction of the nation.

Somers sailed again, and in due time reported to the admiral, who was then waiting for the army, in order to make the second attack. A tremendous gale delayed the expedition; but on the 13th of January, the bombardment of Fort Fisher was commenced, and the military force was landed on Federal Point. A detachment of sailors from the Firefly, under the command of Lieutenant Longstone, was sent on shore to join the naval brigade, and the steamer was variously employed during the action, rendering valuable aid with her hundred pounder, as well as performing various duties, for which her great speed and light draught peculiarly fitted her.

The zeal and energy of Somers were warmly commended, though he had no opportunity to render any signal service in the attack.

Fort Fisher fell this time; every man and every ship was faithful; and though some were distinguished by gallant exploits, the victory was the result of the steadiness of the whole line, rather than of the brilliant deeds of the few. The last maritime stronghold of the rebellion was reduced, and the sinking Confederacy was shut in from all material support from abroad. Its days were numbered, and many of its most rabid supporters were now crying out for peace.

The flag of the Union floated over Fort Fisher, and the great fleet before its shattered ramparts celebrated the victory with clouds of gay flags, with flights of rockets, and with salvos of artillery. It was a glorious day for that expedition. Admiral Porter and General Terry won a glorious fame and an unfading name upon the anuals of their country.

Gallant old Tom Longstone was wounded in the arm in an attempt to rally the sailors when they broke under the most terrible fire that mortal men ever breasted. Lieutenant Longstone did all that any officer could do, but the whole garrison seemed to be gathered at the point where the naval assault was made. The sailors were repulsed and driven back. They had never been disciplined to this kind of work; yet they fought like tigers, hand to hand oftentimes, with the foe; and though they were forced back, even while the American flag was floating over the other side of the works, it was no disgrace to them. Tom stood by to the last, though he was severely wounded, and finally had the satisfaction of beholding a complete triumph. The soldiers did wonders on that day — the sailors hardly less.

With other vessels of light draught the Firefly went up the river, fishing up torpedoes, transporting soldiers, and hammering down rebel batteries, and continued upon this duty until General Terry marched into the deserted city of Wilmington, and raised the national flag where the emblem of treason had insulted the free air for four long years.

The Firefly was ordered to the James River, in the vicinity of which the last groan of the expiring monster of Rebellion was soon to be heard; and on the 20th of March she was on her winding way up the stream. In the mean time Charleston had fallen; negro troops patrolled her streets, and the people of this foul nest of secession were suffering the agonies of actual subjugation. Sherman, with his grand army, was " marching on " in his resistless course, with hardly a foe to impede his exultant march. Columbia, the proud capital of arrogant South Carolina, yielded. and the people repented their folly in the ashes of the burning city. Johnston was retreating before his invincible conqueror, and the whole military power of the rebellion east of Mississippi was concentrated within an area of not more than a hundred and fifty miles.

The movements of General Grant before Petersburg commenced; and his great army, now animated by the sure prestige of victory, was hurled against the rebel lines. The shock was tremendous; the whole world seemed to be shaken by it, for it was the onslaught of freedom, striking its last terrible blow at the legions of slavery.

The fleet on the James was busily employed in fishing up torpedoes, in guarding the pontoons across the river, and in "neutralizing" the enemy's iron-clads which lay above the obstructions. The Firefly found abundant occupation, though there was no opportunity for brilliant and startling achievements; but she bore her full share in the hard work and disagreeable drudgery of the occasion.

Tom Longstone had entirely recovered from his wound; and being a practical man himself, he was the life of every working party sent out from the ship. The old man was an immense favorite with the sailors; for, unlike many who have risen from a low position to a high, he was kind and considerate, while he exacted the full measure of duty from all. He was no tyrant, and had a heart for every man, whatever his degree.

"Well, Mr. Longstone, we have got almost to the end of the rebellion," said Captain Somers, on one of those last days of March, when the roar from beyond Petersburg was heavier than usual.

"No doubt of that, captain," replied Tom. "I shall be a boatswain again before long."

"Do you dread the time?"

"No, sir; far be it from me. I wouldn't prolong the war a single day, if that day would make me an admiral."

"Only one day, Tom?" said Somers, with a smile.

"Not one, sir!" repeated the veteran, with emphasis. "For on that day a husband or a father, a brother or a son, might be killed, and I should be a murderer before God."

"What do you think of those, then, that began this war?"

"They are murderers! The blood of every man who has been killed in this war on both sides rests on their heads. I'd rather be Cain than Jeff Davis, or any other man of his crew."

"I think you are right, Tom."

"As for me, it don't make much difference whether I'm a boatswain or an admiral. This old hulk won't stand many more storms; and I wouldn't do a mean thing for the sake of living twenty years. Well, well," sighed the veteran, as he glanced in the direction from which the roar of the artillery came, "many a good fellow will lose the number of his mess to-day."

"Hundreds of them."

And so the reports of the succeeding days assured them. The rebels had stormed and temporarily possessed themselves of Fort Steadman. The terrible conflict was opened in earnest; and from that time, swarms of prisoners were sent forward to the river, which were guarded by detachments of sailors and marines from the fleet.

For three days the storm of war continued to howl in the distance, and on the peaceful Sabbath more fiercely than before. Vague rumors were flying through the fleet, and everybody felt that the end was at hand. Somers retired as usual that night; but in the first watch, Tom Longstone came down to him with report of great lights and heavy explosions in the direction of Richmond.

The rebels were evacuating the city, blowing up their iron-clads, and firing the town. Richmond, which had defied the armies of the Union for four years, had fallen. The heroic and persevering Grant had struck a blow miles away, which tumbled down the last stronghold of treason. Jeff Davis and his cabinet were fugitives now, fleeing from men, while the wrath of God pursued where men could not reach them.

The morning came, and with it the glad tidings of victory, which foreshadowed peace. The Firefly was ordered to move up the river, and she went up into waters where a loyal steamer had not floated for four years. The negro troops were even then marching through the streets of Richmond. The note of rejoicing, begun in the early morning, was continued through the day. The brightest flags and the heaviest guns proclaimed the joyful event.

The Firefly went up to Varina, and then returned. This river was clear; there was no sign of an enemy upon its waters. At City Point the sounds of rejoicing thrilled upon the ear of soldier and sailor. Cheer upon cheer rent the air, gun upon gun roared the pæan of triumph, and every heart beat in unison with the glad acclaim.

"Glory, hallelujah!" shouted Somers, on the quarter deck of the Firefly, as she passed through the fleet.

"Glory, hallelujah!" returned all who heard him.

Three rousing cheers, such as Jack only can give, came from the flag-ship, as the Firefly ran under her counter.

"What's that?" asked Somers — for there seemed to be something unusual going on.

Calling his gig, he went on board the flag-ship to report the result of his visit up the river. On the quarter deck he discovered a familiar face, which thrilled his heart with delight. It was "Brave Old Salt."

Somers approached the vice admiral, cap in hand, and was immediately recognized.

"Mr. Somers, I am delighted to see you!" said the admiral, extending his hand.

"Thank you, sir," replied the young commander. "This is an unexpected happiness to me."

"There is only one joy to-day, Mr. Somers," continued the admiral. "Richmond has fallen, and the rebellion is ended!"

"Glory, hallelujah!" said Somers, waving his cap.

"I came down here to learn what Grant was doing. God bless him! He has done everything," added the admiral.

Rear Admiral Porter now ordered the Firefly to be placed at the disposal of the Old Salamander, and Somers was happy in the duty assigned to him. A twelve-oar barge received the vice admiral, and conveyed him to the steamer in which his voyage was to be continued. When he was on board, the barge was towed astern for his use farther up the river.

The Firefly steamed up the river with her illustrious passenger, and at the invitation of the admiral, Somers accompanied him to Richmond.

A day later came President Lincoln in a barge, attended by Admiral Porter, and Somers had the honor of being formally presented to the chief magistrate of the nation, who had a pleasant word for him, as he had for all who approached him. Somers assisted in the ovation to the president, and listened with wonder and delight to the shouts of the negroes, as they greeted the author of the Emancipation Proclamation as the saviour and redeemer of their race.

Ten days later, that simple, great man fell by the hand of the assassin, though not till the news of the surrender of Lee's army had gladdened his heart, and assured him that the great work of his lifetime was finished.

Somers was shocked, stunned by the fearful news, the more so that he had so recently pressed the hand of the illustrious martyr; and though the nation was full of mourners, there were none more sincere in their grief than the young commander of the Firefly. He wept as he would have wept for his own father; and shutting himself up in his cabin, in solemn fast, he read his Bible and prayed for the land he loved. How many true souls did the same, when they heard of the awful tragedy!

The war was ended. A few days later came the news of Johnston's surrender. One by one, the gunboats were ordered north, and in June the Firefly dropped her anchor off the navy yard at Charlestown. A few hours later Somers was in the arms of the loved ones at home, weeping tears of joy that the sound of strife was no more heard in the land.

The Firefly was no longer needed in the navy, and with a hundred others she was sold. As soon as she went out of commission, Tom Longstone, having been "honorably discharged with the thanks of the department" as an ensign, returned to his former rank of boatswain. When he obtained a furlough, he paid a visit to Pinchbrook, where he was kindly received by all the friends of his *protégé*. The old man had money enough to buy him a farm and retire from the navy; but he obstinately refused to do so while Somers retained his commission. He confidently expected to be appointed boatswain of the ship to which Lieutenant Somers might be ordered.

During his absence Somers had received occasional letters from Kate Portington; and we will not undertake to say how many reams of fine note paper he spoiled in saying what can be of interest to none but the parties concerned. Of course there was any quantity of liquid moonshine spread out on these dainty sheets, and the young man was all the happier for writing it, as she was for reading it, for Kate and Somers had come to an excellent understanding with each other on these matters.

At the earliest day the public service would admit, he hastened to Newport; but on his arrival he found the commodore's house filled with grief and lamentation. The husband and the father — the kindest of husbands and the tenderest of fathers — had been suddenly stricken down in New Orleans, where his ship was stationed. The sad tidings had come but a few hours before; and a few hours later it had flashed all over the land that one of the nation's truest defenders had fallen at the post of duty.

In her grief Kate clung to Somers, who became the tenderest of comforters. Then she learned, when earth was dark to her, what a wealth of holy hope and pious faith there was in the soul of him she had chosen from the whole world to lean upon in joy and in sorrow, in prosperity and adversity, till life's fitful dream was over. Fondly she looked up to him in her heavy affliction, and through him to the heaven of which he spoke. He wept with her for him who was gone, and if she had loved him before, she reverenced him now.

Two weeks after the news came a steamer bearing the remains of the deceased commodore. Then the tears broke out afresh, and Somers continued to perform the holy office he had chosen. With the bereaved child — the only one — he stood at the tomb, and helped her to see the glory that streamed forth beyond its dark portals. Every day, for weeks after, he visited her, never now to speak of his own selfish heart yearnings, but to utter words of peace and hope. When he announced his intention to return home, she could not restrain her tears, so needful had he become to her in the depth of her sorrow.

In the autumn her mother and herself came to Boston to spend the winter. Kate was cheerful now, but the affliction through which she had passed had given a shade of pensive sadness to her beautiful face, which time alone could wear away. They attended the wedding of Major

Somers, John's brother, and rejoiced with him as he put the cup of bliss to his lips. Lilian and Kate became fast friends; they were nearer alike now than before the death of Commodore Portington.

The winter passed away, and early in March Lieutenant Somers was appointed to a ship bound to the Pacific Ocean. He must be absent two or three years. He hastened to Kate with the intelligence; and sad as it was to himself, he knew it would be infinitely more so to her. She turned pale, and burst into tears. Her mother was hardly less affected.

"You must not go, John! O, no! You will not leave me!"

"I must obey orders."

"You can resign," suggested Mrs. Portington.

"Resign!" exclaimed Somers. "Resign when I am ordered to difficult or disagreeable duty."

"You need not make so much of it," added the matron, with a smile. "There are twice as many officers in the navy as are required. It is certainly no disgrace, in time of peace, to resign. You will only make a place for another who wants to visit the Pacific."

"You must resign, John," pleaded Kate, with an eloquence which he could not resist.

"On one condition I will do so," replied he, at last. "If there should be war, I shall return to my post, if needed."

And thus it was that Somers left the navy. His prize money, which had been carefully invested from time to time by Captain Barney, now amounted to more than twenty thousand dollars. He was able to retire, and he did so.

It is generally understood that they are to be married in the autumn, when Mr. Somers will receive half a million with his wife, who is worth a million times that sum herself. As the happy event has not yet occurred, we have nothing to say about it, but we wish them every joy in anticipation. Mrs. Portington speaks hopefully of the occasion, and has already selected a location, in the vicinity of Boston, where the happy young couple are to reside.

This event has decided Tom Longstone. He has thrown up his warrant, and bought a farm in Pinchbrook, on which he intends to "lay up" for the rest of his life. A niece, who lost her husband in the war, is his housekeeper, and at the time of Somers's last visit, the veteran was at the high tide of felicity.

With many regrets we bid adieu to John Somers, to Thomas his brother, and all of the family. We leave them prosperous and happy; but they have purchased earth's joys and heaven's hopes by being faithful to duty — true to God and themselves.

www.ingramcontent.com/pod-product-compliance
Lightning Source LLC
Chambersburg PA
CBHW021213240426
43667CB00038B/397